Our Debt to Greece and Rome

EDITORS

George Depue Hadzsits, Ph.D.

University of Pennsylvania

David Moore Robinson, Ph.D., LL.D.

The Johns Hopkins University

[ii]

THE POETICS OF ARISTOTLE
ITS MEANING AND INFLUENCE

BY
LANE COOPER

PROFESSOR OF THE ENGLISH LANGUAGE AND LITERATURE
IN CORNELL UNIVERSITY

MARSHALL JONES COMPANY
BOSTON · MASSACHUSETTS

Printed August, 1923

THE PLIMPTON PRESS·NORWOOD·MASSACHUSETTS
PRINTED IN THE UNITED STATES OF AMERICA

TO

JOHN ADAMS SCOTT

PROFESSOR OF GREEK IN NORTHWESTERN UNIVERSITY

WHO JOINS WITH ARISTOTLE IN THE DEFENCE OF HOMER

CONTENTS

[vii]

PREFACE

It is only less difficult to write a popular book about the *Poetics* of Aristotle than to write one about the *Elements* of Euclid. Yet I trust the following pages give an intelligible account of what Aristotle tried to say in his book on poetry, and how writers in various ages have reacted to his thoughts.

In dealing with such a topic in limited space I could not avoid omissions. I am conscious that the expert reader will miss not a few names of scholars and poets who have studied the *Poetics*; and that in order to make clear the significance of Italian criticism, and to give at least reasonable attention to the *Poetics* in English literature, I have had to dispose of the French critics, an endless subject, in summary fashion.

From the nature of the series in which this volume appears, I can give nothing like a full account of my indebtedness for various items in my book. I owe a large debt to the works of Bywater and Spingarn, an appreciable debt to those of Saintsbury and Gregory Smith, and something to the recent acute and stimulating researches of Gudeman and Gillet. Of materials not generally accessible I should especially mention the paper by Gudeman, *The Influence of Aristotle's Poetics on Modern Literature*, read by the Secretary at a meeting of the Classical Club, Philadelphia, Nov. 5, 1920; the Secretary was good enough to send me the minutes of that meeting, which contain an abstract of the paper. To Professor Gillet my thanks are due not only for copies of his published articles on topics related to the *Poetics*, and for information communicated in his letters, but also for his added kindness in reading and criticizing my manuscript before it was submitted to the editors of the series. I wish also to thank my friend and colleague Professor Joseph Q. Adams for his criticism of the manuscript.

THE POETICS OF ARISTOTLE
ITS MEANING AND INFLUENCE

THE
POETICS OF ARISTOTLE
ITS MEANING AND INFLUENCE

I. CHARACTER, ANTECEDENTS, AND GENERAL SCOPE OF THE POETICS

THE *Poetics* of Aristotle is brief, at first sight hard and dry, and yet one of the most illuminating and influential books ever produced by the sober human mind. After twenty-two centuries it remains the most stimulating and helpful of all analytical works dealing with poetry—and poetry is the most vital and lasting achievement of man. This pregnant treatise, dating from some time before the year 323 B. C., is indeed short and condensed. Castelvetro's famous 'exposition' of it (Vienna, 1570) fills 768 pages, and runs to something like 384,000 words. The *Poetics* itself contains perhaps 10,000 words. In the great Berlin edition of Aristotle (1831) it takes up only 30 columns of print, or 15 pages; in the

last notable edition of the *Poetics,* that of Bywater (1909), the text occupies 45 pages out
of 431. The *Poetics* makes about a hundredth
part of the extant works of Aristotle.

Though never long, it doubtless once was
longer; and it probably was associated with
another work of Aristotle, now represented
only by fragments, his dialogue *On Poets,* and
with his *Homeric Problems.* In the same
group of writings were the *Peplos* and the
Didascaliæ, the latter a history or record of
the Greek dramatic contests, with the names
of victors and similar data. The dialogue
On Poets seems to have been of a more literary
character. At all events the *Poetics* does not
now resemble the finished work of that Aristotle whose style was praised by Cicero and
Quintilian. What we have of it may be the
notes that served the master through various
years for some part of his lectures; such notes
he would expand in oral discussion, adding examples, reconciling apparent contradictions,
solving difficulties with his pupils in the Peripatetic fashion. The defence of Homer toward
the end of the book connects it with the *Problems,* and the last chapter, on the relative
merits of epic and tragic poetry, has the look

[4]

of an embryo dialogue. Or we may have in the *Poetics* the notes of some person who attended Aristotle's lectures and colloquies—a hypothesis that would explain omissions and discrepancies that troubled the last generation of modern scholars. Or, finally, the work may be the grudging abstract by some student of the Alexandrian age or later, who took the essentials from one book or section by the master, and therewith joined what seemed important or germane from one or two others. There may have been several steps in the reduction of the *Poetics* to its present state, which it had reached some time before the sixth century A.D. If so, the history of the treatise would resemble that of Greek learning as a whole in the gradual decay of scholarship and science, until in the Dark Ages the rich and detailed investigations of the Alexandrian period—in biology, for example—had dwindled to the barest epitomes. There is at least one unexpected gap in our *Poetics*. The treatise does not fulfil its own promise regarding a discussion of comedy; certain scholars have found the promise redeemed in a fragment known as the *Tractatus Coislinianus*, the merest outline, descended from a body of critical doctrine, now lost, of wider range than the extant *Poetics*.

We have no adequate knowledge about the composition of Aristotle's works in literary criticism. His *Rhetoric*, though the text is now corrupt, fared better in the Græco-Roman world than the *Poetics*, meeting the practical needs of Roman orators. We do not know when either treatise was written, yet there has been a tendency to regard the *Poetics* as the earlier. Doubtless both existed side by side during some part of Aristotle's activity as teacher, and underwent occasional revision at his hands. After his death the *Rhetoric* was included in a body of like treatises, now mostly of uncertain origin. But the *Poetics* is the only technical discussion of its subject that has come down to us from ancient Greece. For the study of Greek art, including poetic art, it is, after the masterpieces themselves, the most valuable document we have from antiquity.

In its own time, however, it was not a solitary work; and it had predecessors as well as contemporaries in its field. Here Aristotle did not, as in the *Topica*, feel that he labored as a pioneer, but had models on which to

[6]

improve. In *Poetics* 8 he suggests that Homer
may have worked with conscious art. If a
full-fledged theory of rhetoric came from the
Sicilian to the Athenian orators, why, we may
ask, should not a theory of the poetic art come
to the Athenian drama, if not from Sicily, then
from Asia Minor—from Miletus or Smyrna—
along with a body of epic tradition that fur-
nished subject-matter for the Attic stage? The
more we learn of early Ægean culture, and
of its persistence at the Sicilian and Ionian
fringes when the centre was swept away, the
greater seems the debt of Athens to that culture for the seeds of art and science. Some
notions of Homeric rules of art, accordingly,
may have drifted down to the predecessors of
Aristotle with the *Iliad* and the *Odyssey*. In
the *Republic* Plato makes Socrates speak of
the 'ancient quarrel between philosophy and
poetry.' How early did the naughty Homeric
tales of the gods, of Mars and Venus, become
a topic of debate between moralist and literary
critic? The *Poetics* notes that Xenophanes (*fl.*
530 B. C.) thought them very bad, and implic-
itly takes issue with the *Republic* for likewise
condemning them with no appeal to standards
of art.

[7]

But the foregoing are vaguer considerations. There is evidence in Plato's *Phœdrus,* as in the *Poetics,* that Sophocles consciously observed dramatic laws. And, among other sayings, he declared that Æschylus 'did right without knowing why'; he himself, then, composed aright, *knowing why.* The *Poetics* records a maxim of Agathon on dramatic probability; and indeed, in acting and staging their plays, and in training the chorus and actors, the tragic poets must have reflected much on their art. That the great dramatists had a store of reflections is evinced by Aristophanes' *Frogs,* which in effect is the work of a great literary critic, and shows the poet to be familiar with tragic technique, and with stock terms and methods of criticism; his comic purpose should not blind us to his actual knowledge. Another (lost) play of Aristophanes was itself called *Pœesis,* while of his contemporaries Plato (not the philosopher) produced a *Poet* and *Poets,* and Nicochares likewise a *Poet.* These comedies were the forerunners of those with similar titles in the age of Aristotle: *Poets* and *Poetry* by Alexis, *Pœesis* by Antiphanes, and a *Poet* each by Biottus and Phœnicides.

[8]

In prose, it has been assumed that the Dialogues of Plato were background and incentive to the treatise of Aristotle; it is often held that the *Poetics* is a defence of poetry against the attacks of Socrates upon Homer and the dramatists in Books 2, 3, and 10 of the *Republic*. But the prose background was larger. The circle to which Plato belonged was a group of theorists and investigators,[1] including botanists, students of biology, of grammar, of music—of art and science in general. Among other disciples of Socrates, we find Crito, Simmias of Thebes, and Simon, who produced, according to Diogenes Laertius, works discussing poetry and fine art. Of uncertain date, but a precursor of Aristotle, was a Democritus who wrote a treatise *On Poetry* and another on *Rhythms and Harmony*. And again, of the members of the Platonic school, Speusippus dealt with rhetoric and art, while Xenocrates wrote on oratorical and literary problems; the learned Heracleides of Pontus wrote on music, and on poetry and the poets. In the *Poetics* Aristotle himself alludes a dozen times or more to critical treatises bearing on his subject; he mentions by name the authors Protagoras, Hippias of Thasos, Eucleides,

[9]

Glaucon, and Ariphrades. Their works are lost; his alone remains, if not as he might have chosen to leave it for posterity, yet in a shape by which the world has benefited, and can benefit more. We may suppose that from this body of writings he as usual eliminated the chaff, and reorganized the essentials, synthesizing, emphasizing, subordinating, filling out in a large and luminous perspective. Through him we probably owe much to his contemporaries and predecessors.

At the same time the *Poetics* must be thought an original work, based upon observation and comparison of many narrative poems, and a thousand Greek dramas of which we now have but a fraction. Our author had an ample assortment of cases for study. And though he took all knowledge for his province, neglecting perhaps no subject cultivated by the Greeks save geography, though he brought to the analysis of poetic art a mind exercised in philosophy, ethics, politics, logic, psychology, and rhetoric, we should remember that he was the son of a physician, had himself a medical training, and was, if one thing more than another, what we call a biologist. He is interested in life and the principles of life. He

[10]

therefore studies poetry, a form of life, as a philosophical and also a specialized anatomist and physiologist. He considers its structure and its function. Above all is he concerned with the function and ultimate purpose of it. The common mistake of unoriginal students, in our day as in his, has been to dissect a poem—a complete organism—without regard to the meaning and purpose of the whole. It is the mistake of pedants who divide a masterpiece, and do not rejoin the parts in living union; and thus their pupils, who love life, come to hate the work—of Milton, say—that they are 'studying.' But the originality of Aristotle helps us to relive the life of Greek epic and dramatic poetry. Dry (not dull) though his treatise may at first appear, I have yet to meet the student, mature enough to grasp the outline of a narrative or a drama, whose interest can not be quickened by applying to the narrative or drama the Aristotelian principles of life and art.

The *Poetics* does not merely help us to appreciate the few Greek dramas that survive, to imagine the other Greek critical treatises from which it partly sprang, and to feel that almost every critical problem our minds conceive was broached by the Greeks; it also tells us much concerning the vast body of Greek dramas that are lost, and yields much of our information regarding Greek stage-practice. We have but 7 whole plays by Æschylus, who is said to have written from 70 to 90; but 7 by Sophocles, who is credited with 123; and but 18 or (with the *Rhesus*) 19 by Euripides, who wrote perhaps 92. Of late, considerable fragments have been regained of an eighth play, the *Trackers,* by Sophocles. Of the 160 plays by Chœrilus, somewhat earlier than Æschylus, we know almost nothing. Of tragedy in Aristotle's own lifetime we have possibly one example, the *Rhesus,* if that is not by Euripides. Yet, including the fifty plays which his own friend Theodectes produced with conspicuous success, Aristotle could easily have read, from those of Chœrilus down, well over a thousand Greek tragedies. Most of these, when we hear of them at all, are to us little more than names; some, at best, survive in chance fragments of a few lines only. Then, in addition to the 11 plays of Aristophanes that have come down to us, Aristotle must have known the lost works of that author, not to mention other poets of the Old

Comedy, such as Cratinus and Eupolis, or the
mass of plays in the age succeeding—the so-
called Middle Comedy, which we must mainly
judge by the quotations in Athenæus.

But we should not expect too much from
the *Poetics*. The treatise as its stands tells
us little about Greek Comedy. And if we go
to it for light on poetry as this is vaguely
conceived by modern readers we shall be dis-
appointed. Nowadays people think of poetry
as versified composition about vernal flowers
and the breath of 'nature.' When they meet
lyrical effusions like Tennyson's *Crossing the
Bar,* or Wordsworth's *Tintern Abbey,* or anything else in which they hear of the human
soul being reabsorbed into the world-soul, or of
'a motion and a spirit . . . that rolls through
all things'—in other words, when they meet
the notion of divine immanence lyrically expressed, when they meet versified Neoplato-
nism—readers think they have found true
poetry. For the treatise of Aristotle, however, poetry is epic poetry (as Homer is the
greatest poet) or dramatic poetry (as tragedy
is the noblest poetical type). Aristotle does,
indeed, consider the choral odes of tragedy,
but not apart from the drama. Had he chosen

[13]

to examine what we call the lyric, as a separate form, he probably would have done so, not in a treatise on poetry, but in one on music; though to him, as to the Greeks in general, the activities of poet and musical composer were not far apart. In the days of Æschylus, Sophocles, and Aristophanes, a poet wrote both words and music for his drama. The author of the *Poetics,* coming later, does not boast of a very thorough musical education.

II. CONTENTS OF THE POETICS

WHAT, then, does the *Poetics* contain? The treatise now consists of 26 chapters of varied length, a division probably made after Aristotle's time for more convenient reference in his works. But we may preferably divide the whole into four sections (chapters 1–5, 6–22, 23–24, 25–26), of which the first is introductory. Aristotle proposes to discuss the poetic art in general, and the kinds of poetry according to the function of each, explaining how a tragedy or an epic poem should be constructed in order to produce the right effect upon an audience or reader. Since he regards a work of art as a living organism, he likens each several kind of poetry, and indeed each individual poem, to an animal, and will consider its ideal form or structure as related to the proper end or function of the art. In the first section, therefore, he treats of epic poetry, tragedy, and comedy, under the general notion of imitative art. What Aristotle means by 'imitation' or 'imitative art' must wait for a later explanation, since his technical term has a meaning far different from the general sense to which the modern reader is used. In the second section, tragedy is defined, in a sentence every phrase of which has been subject to a vast amount of learned comment, and the principles of its construction are treated in detail. In the third section we turn to epic poetry and the principles of its construction—what it has in common with tragedy, and wherein the two differ. The fourth section deals with problems in criticism and the principles of their solution; in a measure it is a defence of poetry, and a reply to the critics of Homer. The last problem concerns the relative excellence of epic poetry and tragedy. To Aristotle, while Homer is the greatest poet, tragedy, in the hands of Sophocles, is the noblest form of poetic art.

Such, in general outline or main content, is the extant *Poetics*. Is there any place in the scheme for a detailed treatment of comedy? Our expectations are aroused in the first section by the conjoined names of Homer, Sophocles, and Aristophanes as representative in their several kinds of art, and by a promise that comedy will be examined later; but the promise is not adequately fulfilled in our treatise. Is the so-called *Tractatus Coislinianus* (first printed in 1839 [2]) at least partly derived from a lost portion of Aristotle's literary criticism? Therein the forms of the ludicrous are sketched by the hand of a masterly critic, who had grasped the secret of Aristophanic comedy. But of this hereafter. Let us first run over the substance of the *Poetics* in more detail.[3]

That is not an easy task. The work is packed with thoughts, and every thought is full of energy and suggestion. And, partly because many phrases are like hints to be expanded in a lecture, with brief indications of examples, partly because of corruptions in our text, there are various points in the work upon which scholars have not agreed. Furthermore, in order to be brief, I must tacitly accommodate the following analysis to modern ways of thinking.

Aristotle begins by dividing the genus poetry into its species, the main ones being epic poetry, tragedy, and comedy; and he assumes that a poem is to be judged by its effect upon a man of sound sense and good education, though not necessarily an expert—upon the 'judicious,' as Hamlet remarks. A properly constructed tragedy will not offend the judicious. Form and function being virtually interchangeable terms, a well-formed poem, like a beautiful living animal, will give the right sort of judge the right kind of pleasure.

The various species of poetry are modes of 'imitation.' That is, the poet, like the painter, the musician, the sculptor, has in mind a conception which he will represent for his own and others' delight. A painter wishes to represent a man. The result is not a man of flesh and blood, but an 'imitation' of a man in line and color on a flat surface. The sculptor likewise has a mental image which he 'imitates' in marble, and the musician a sentiment or feeling which he 'imitates' in melody and rhythm. The conception which the artist 'imitates' is his 'object'; the pigments, or the stone, or the notes, in which he represents his object, we call the 'medium.' Or again, Greek dancers, like our Russian dancers, 'imitated' human emotions and states of feeling by rhythmical motions and postures of the body. So the dramatist, using words, musical notes, and the evolutions of a dancing chorus as his 'medium,' represents the characters, actions,

[18]

and experiences of men as his 'object.' But
whether the artist be a dramatic or an epic
poet, we may say, in brief, that his 'object'
is 'men in action' (doing or suffering), and
his principal 'medium' spoken language. He
holds the mirror up to human nature. A
dramatist 'imitates' the actions of men directly,
presenting them as if actually occurring before
our eyes, while an epic poet 'imitates' them
indirectly, in the manner of a tale that is told.
Further, one art, as tragedy, may represent
its 'object,' men in action, as nobler than men
commonly are, and another art, as comedy,
may represent them as less noble. The 'imitative' arts, then, may differ as regards the
objects, the media, or the manner of 'imitation.'

Aristotle's word for 'imitative' we may trans-
late by 'mimetic' also; the Greek term suggests
to him, among other things, the Greek *mime*,
and prose dialogues generally, without the
metrical and other embellishments of epic
poetry and tragedy. Aristotle recognizes the
poetic or 'mimetic' quality of the farcical prose
dramas of Sophron and the Dialogues of Plato,
though he would hardly call a dramatic 'imitation' of men a poem, if metrical language were
absent. He does clearly say that metrical

[19]

composition is not the distinguishing feature of a poet: you might turn Herodotus, or a scientific treatise, into verse, and you would not have a poem. Yet the Homeric tale of Achilles is all the more beautiful for the hexameters in which the imitation is worked out, and tragedy and comedy gain much from the added beauties of metre, song, and dance. Metre does, in fact, come under the general head of rhythm, rhythmical language being a genus, and metres being species of it; and rhythm is also found in the speeches and songs of the drama.

In his digression, then, Aristotle regards metre, not as essential, but as a recognized adjunct of poetry. The principle of imitation being essential, the embodiment in metrical or non-metrical language is a secondary consideration. But we must not infer that rhythm, in the wider sense, is of little consequence to the poet. For the sort of 'imitation' that embraces the Platonic Dialogues and prose dramas, Aristotle says he finds no technical name; modern writers like Shelley will use 'poetry' as a generic term covering the rhythmical language of Plato and the Bible as well as the verse of Homer, Dante, and Milton.

In German, *dichtung* stands for imaginative writing of every sort, while *dichter* rather applies to one who writes in verse.

Aristotle's next digression concerns the etymology of *drama,* and the claims of the Dorians, as against Athens, to the invention of both tragedy and comedy. One or more earlier writers must have held that *dramas,* comic and tragic, were so called because in both we have imitations of men acting and *doing,* and because, it was alleged, the verb *dran* ('to do'), which reappears in the noun *drama,* at one time belonged to the Dorian rather than the Attic dialect. There seems also to have been a discussion touching the origin of comedy. Did it begin in Dorian Megara or Dorian Syracuse? It did not originate in Athens, so ran the argument, for Epicharmus, who came from Syracuse, preceded the earliest comic poets of Attica. Aristotle is but moderately interested in such discussions; he does not try to settle the conflicting claims—though from them we may gather hints of the artistic debt of Athens to Syracuse; he is occupied with the notion that drama directly presents characters that live and move before our eyes. He gives no derivation of the word *tragedy,* which seems to mean 'goat-song,' that is, a performance of men originally disguised as satyrs; and sanctions no derivation of the word *comedy,* 'comus-song,' which is connected with the Greek verb *comazein,* 'to revel'—with the Comus, or wandering dance of the Phallic worshipers.

He is deeply interested, however, in the psychological origins of art. Poetry, art in general, results from native tendencies in mankind. Of the human qualities that must originally have produced art, the first is the impulse to imitate, a habit pervading the animate world, but most notable in man, for he is more imitative than any other creature. The rest act rather by instinct, while man learns at first by imitation, and so he advances more and more in accomplishment. Thus, we may add, children display the artistic and imitative impulse when, as little actors, they improvise their games and naïve dramas. Secondly, there is the natural pleasure we all take in observing acts or products of imitation. As adults or children love to enact a drama, so they love to watch its production. Aristotle's instance, drawn from the realm of painting, we may concretely render thus:

[22]

Even when the object imitated is repulsive—
as a toad, or a corpse—we delight in the work
of the artist who represents the object faith-
fully. One thinks of Aristophanes' *Frogs,* and
of the monstrous beetle in his *Peace,* or of the
cadaver in Rembrandt's *Lesson in Anatomy.*
We may dislike the things, but the 'imitations'
give artistic pleasure; and, says Aristotle, for
a reason. They satisfy the universal desire
to learn, for, among human pleasures, that
of learning is the keenest. Men even of
limited capacity enjoy looking at a portrait,
since in the act of observing it they acquire
knowledge and draw inferences. When we
say, 'Why, that is So-and-so!' we have made
an inference, and feel a corresponding pleasure.

Again, there is in man a natural instinct
for music and rhythm—and under the head of
rhythm, we note, fall the several species of
metre. In the beginning, then, being possessed
of the impulse to imitate, and a sense of
harmony and rhythm, men originated poetry,
at first in naïve improvisations; and then
gradually, in the main by slight advances,
progressed until they gave rise to an art.

But we quickly notice a division in the art;
for some men are by nature more grave, and

some are less; and hence in early times the graver spirits would represent noble actions, while the meaner would affect the doings of the ignoble. Thus on one side we should have hymns and panegyrics, and on the other, lampoons; though Aristotle can mention no poem of the latter sort before Homer, he thinks there must have been many such, and, beginning with the Homeric *Margites*, knows of various examples. In the early poems of this kind, its suitability brought in an iambic metre, and so *iambic* has come to mean 'satirical'—because poets formerly lampooned, or *iambized*, one another in this metre. Of the early poets, accordingly, some became authors of iambic verse, and others of heroic.

But Homer surpassed his fellows in either class. In the serious vein he is pre-eminent, not only through the general excellence of his work, but through his dramatic quality as well, since he makes his personages live before us. And likewise in the comic vein: in the *Margites* he did not produce invective, but rendered the ludicrous dramatic, thereby marking out the general lines of comedy.

When tragedy and comedy arose, however, the poets with a bent for lower subjects no longer took to lampooning, but went in for comedy; and the graver spirits no longer became epic poets, but producers of tragedy. And the reason was that the newer forms were more impressive, and were held in greater esteem.

Thus succinctly does Aristotle sketch the growth of the poetic art from its first beginnings. Assuming, now, that tragedy as a whole has reached the stage of a mature art, he dismisses, as not germane to his inquiry, the question whether any of its elements (as the choral part) is capable of further development. But he does briefly consider the origin and progress of the drama, in a measure relying on previous authorities.

Both tragedy and comedy originated in improvisations. Tragedy goes back to the improvising leader of the dithyrambic satyr-chorus, in the Bacchic procession; comedy to the leaders of the Phallic song and dance, likewise a Bacchic ceremony—surviving, as he notes, in many places. From its crude beginnings tragedy progressed little by little, successive authors improving on their forerunners, until at length it attained its proper form. Of the changes in a long development, Aristotle

mentions but a few main ones. Strange to
say, he does not name Thespis. He notes
that, from the single primitive spokesman,
Æschylus increased the number of actors to
two, reducing the amount of choral chanting,
and making spoken dialogue the main thing.
Then Sophocles, who introduced painted scen-
ery, increased the actors to three; be it noted
that one actor could assume more than one
rôle in a play. And as tragedy got farther
away from the satyr-dance, the little plots and
grotesque diction of the earlier type gave way
to a greater action and more elevated style,
while the trochaic metre, suited to dancing,
yielded to an iambic measure, suited—in Greek
as in English—to the rhythm of spoken discourse. Lastly, Aristotle marks an increase
in the number of episodes in the action. As
for other details, such as the development of
costume, he thinks it would be a long and
needless task to pursue them. And on the
early history of comedy Aristotle's sources tell
him little, since comedy was late in becoming
a matter of public concern; the magistrate
did not provide the comic poet with a chorus
until 487 B. C.; the type had taken shape by
the time there began to be records of the

contests.   Aristotle consulted such records, but must have learned from historians or critics that the framing of comic plots was accredited to Epicharmus and Phormis, and hence originated, not at Athens, but in Sicily.   He notes, as very important, that, of Athenian poets, Crates first discarded personal abuse as a means to laughter, and produced generalized comic actions.   In this tendency I believe he regards Crates as a precursor of Aristophanes; the plots of the *Birds* and the *Plutus* are 'generalized.'

For Aristotle, the general framework of a comedy was doubtless the main consideration, comedy being an 'imitation' of an action carried on by men of inferior moral bent.   The agents, however, should be faulty only in so far as their shortcomings are ludicrous, the ludicrous being but a species, not all, of the genus ugly.   It is that kind of shortcoming or deformity which causes no pain, and does no harm; thus the comic mask is ludicrous, being ugly and distorted, with no suggestion of pain. So, one might add, the personages and incidents of Aristophanes, who followed Crates, are ridiculous, not painful.   Talkover (Peisthetærus) in the *Birds,* 'Socrates' in the *Clouds,*

[27]

men of inferior bent, are not faulty in every
way; their shortcomings are neither painful
nor corrupting; and the action in each play
is of a general and impersonal sort. The play
does not amount to the direct abuse of a private
individual.

Finally, this opening section of the work
differentiates tragedy and the epic poem. The
two have so much in common: each is an
imitation, in lofty verse, of serious events.
But the epic poem employs one kind of verse,
the hexameter, throughout; whereas tragedy
has a variety of metres. And epic poetry is
in the manner of a tale that is told, while
in tragedy we have an action directly presented. Again, the epic poem is longer than
a tragedy; it is not restricted to any fixed
limit of time. At an earlier stage, says Aristotle, this difference regarding time did not
exist; epic and tragic poets were alike in not
restricting themselves to any special limits.
But, he notes, in his own day (from fifty to
seventy years after Euripides) tragic poets
aim to represent the action as occurring within
twenty-four hours, or at all events try to avoid
exceeding this limit by much. This is all he
has to say in the passage that later gave

the sixteenth-century Italian critics the 'Aristotelian' unity of time. Neither here nor elsewhere does he recommend the observance of this unity; and as for the so-called unity of place, also discussed by the Italians, the *Poetics* does not refer to it. Aristotle also remarks that all the constituent parts of an epic poem are found in tragedy; he means that in both forms there will be (1) a plot, (2) some sort of moral bent in the agents, (3) a display of their way of arguing and inferring, and (4) the use of diction as the 'medium.' But two constituents of tragedy are absent from an epic poem; these are (5) the musical element, and (6) the element of 'spectacle'— all that appeals to the eye when the play is acted. Since tragedy has all the essentials of an epic poem, and two more of its own, it follows that a competent judge of tragedy will know what is good or bad in epic poetry, too.

The second section, on the principles of construction for tragedy, begins with a famous definition. Tragedy is defined in terms (1) of the object imitated—men in action; (2) of the medium of imitation—embellished language; (3) of the manner of imitation—direct presentation; and (4) of the function of tragic art—the arousal and purgation of pity and fear. Thus, save for the last point, the effect, the definition is gathered up from the foregoing chapters: Tragedy is an imitation of an action that is serious, and, having magnitude, complete in itself; in language variously embellished, the several kinds of embellishment being severally used in different parts of the play; in the manner of an action directly presented, not narrated; through pity and fear effecting the proper catharsis of such emotions.

By language variously embellished is meant language that is simply rhythmical or metrical, language that is intoned, and language uttered in song. Some portions of a Greek tragedy, as prologue and episode, were rendered in verse alone, without being sung or chanted; other portions, as parode and stasimon, were sung or chanted. The whole play, of course, was in metre; in delivering it, the actors as well as the chorus employed, by turns, song, speech, and an intermediate recitative like chanting or intoning, which might be accompanied by the clarinet.

Aristotle's catharsis of pity and fear is a simpler matter than the critics have made of

[30]

it. Whatever the effect Sophocles' *Œdipus the King* has on a man of good education and normal sentiment, that is what the *Poetics* means by the catharsis of the tragic emotions. Our suspense as Œdipus nears the fearful disclosure that he has unwittingly slain his father and married his mother, and our pity when he learns the truth, discovers that his mother has destroyed herself, and blinds himself with her brooches—these are the Aristotelian pity and fear. The suspense is thrilling; we shiver with apprehension. When the discovery is complete, the tension is relaxed, and we weep. Our tears are a mark of the catharsis, or relief of emotion. Milton's 'all passion spent,' at the end of *Samson Agonistes,* describes the effect. Aristotle's tragic purgation is not a medical metaphor, but a medico-literary term for an observed fact, one that can be noted in an audience at the presentation of good tragedy, or when the tragedy is read; tears are a bodily secretion, and the relief that follows them is distinct. The catharsis may be violent. There is a tradition that the *Furies* of Æschylus wrought tremendously upon the audience; at the sight of the chorus, with their dreadful masks and snaky locks, boys fainted, and women miscarried. In Aristotle's psychology, the tragic purgation is psycho-physiological; the bodily *motions* are the counterpart of *emotions* in the soul. It seems to have been his view that nearly all of us, and some in particular, are troubled with latent fear and pity; by bringing these emotions to the surface, and discharging them, tragedy affords a harmless relief, which is all the more pleasant and desirable because at the theatre they are not aroused by actual events, but by an *'imitation* of an action.' Further, tragedy has the embellishments of an ornate and rhythmical diction; of music, in which the clarinet has a special value for catharsis; and of 'spectacle,' dignified and awe-inspiring through the rhythmical evolutions of the chorus, the appearance of the gods, and the costume of chorus and actors. Music and 'spectacle' take us back to the primitive satyr-dance; we recall that the drama grew out of Bacchic rites in which the votaries became inspired actors in a wild or frenzied processional dance, and, giving rein to their 'enthusiasm,' spent all their passion, and doubtless ended in a pleasing calm. Aristotle also understood the Greek homeopathic cure of emotional

[32]

disturbance, 'enthusiasm,' by wild and restless music; as, in the Bible, David purges Saul of mania by the music of the harp. Since the tragic purgation was an observed fact, Aristotle may have felt no need of dwelling on the fact itself, as a medical treatise of our day would not dilate upon the act of excretion, but upon the means of producing it. Such is the emphasis of the *Poetics;* although commentators, finding in the *Politics* a statement that the term 'catharsis' would be more fully explained in the *Poetics,* and missing a detailed account of the process in the latter work, believe that a portion of the text is lost. The *Poetics* does take up in full the means by which the purgation should be effected.

From his synthetic definition of tragedy Aristotle proceeds to analyze the elements, six in number, that require separate attention from the poet. Since the action devised by the poet will be performed by persons on the stage, one element will be all that concerns stage-presentation, including costume, setting, and the like. Secondly, there is the composition of the music; and thirdly, the composition in words, the working out of the story in metrical language. Music and diction are the

[33]

medium in which the action is expressed, and the poet must attend to each of them.

Again, the object represented is an action of men, and hence the poet must endow these agents with ethical qualities, each with a habit of choice or way of reacting to a situation; that is, fourthly, he must represent the *ethos* of the *dramatis personæ*. Further, not only must these persons be endowed with a habit of choice, better or worse, but they must be made to think and reason in ways that will appear in their speech and action; so that a fifth element for the poet's consideration is thought (or intellect); for it is from a man's habit of choice, and his way of reasoning, that we ascribe goodness or badness, success or failure, to his acts. As moral bent and manner of reasoning give rise to the particular acts of men, so there are the same two causes of success or failure in a man's career. Thus, since the poet in his drama represents human success or failure, he must provide his agents with a certain disposition of will, to be shown in their choices and refusals, and with a manner of thought, which must appear when they try to prove or disprove a special point, or when they avouch some general truth.

[34]

Sixthly, there is the kernel of the play, the action which the poet imitates; and this he works out in the plot or fable of the tragedy. The plot is that synthesis of incidents which gives form or being to the play as a whole.

In every tragedy there are these six elements, and there can be no others. Upon these the poet bestows his art, and by these, as they are well or ill handled, we judge the total excellence of his work. Two, the musical composition and the composition in language, concern the medium of imitation; one, spectacle, the manner; and three, plot, moral bent, and thought, the objects.

Some difficulty may be felt by the reader because Aristotle does not think of the poet as merely bringing forth characters who sing, discourse in metrical language, and perform certain acts. But Aristotle is right in his separation of the elements that severally demand the care of the dramatist; nor was his analytical method ever more helpful than in distinguishing between the habit of choice (as manifest in the rash or belated acts of Œdipus or Hamlet) and the way in which the personages of a drama generalize and argue. The two elements are as distinct, while as closely

[35]

related, as the subjects of rhetoric and ethics. A poet must see to it that his tragic hero makes a wrong decision at a critical juncture; and also that his personages argue and generalize, prove and disprove, urge and dissuade, as is meet for a given episode and for the outcome of the play.

In Aristotle's view the plot is the most important of the six elements. He does not call it more important than the agents, for he does not regard the agents as a single element; he divides human nature, in life and in dramatic art, into will and intellect, separable things for the constructing poet and the critic. To him, all six elements are indispensable, but the plot of a tragedy demands first attention. We may say that it has the same importance as the plan of a building. Construct this of marble, or construct it of granite; with the same plan you will have essentially the same building. But alter the plan, and you change the very essence of the structure. Aristotle argues thus: Tragedy is an imitation, not of men as such, but of action and life, of happiness and misery; and happiness and misery are not states of being, but forms of activity; the end for which we live is some form of action, not the realization of a moral quality. Men are better or worse according to their moral bent; but they become happy or wretched in their actual deeds. In the drama, consequently, the agents will not do and suffer in order to evince their bent of character; rather, the display of moral bent is included as subsidiary to the things that are done. So that the incidents of the action, and the structural ordering of these incidents, are the end and aim of the tragedy. Here, as in everything else, the final purpose is the main consideration.

In the passage on life and the drama our author rises to a sober eloquence. Very likely the relative importance of 'action' and 'character' was debated in Greek criticism, as it often is now. Aristotle reinforces his position with a paradox: such is the importance of action that, whereas tragedy can not exist without it, one may construct a tragedy in which the agents have no distinctive character —that is, no habit of choice. In fact, he adds, beginning with Euripides, most Greek tragedies are deficient in the element of character, and the defect is common in other poets. Nor is it confined to them, for there is a like

[37]

defect in painters.—One might compare Rembrandt's vigorous delineation of character with the absence of this quality in Rubens. Aristotle is bound to make his point: you may string together a set of speeches well-composed as regards *ethos*, metre, diction, and thought, and yet fail to secure the effect of tragedy; the effect is much more certain with a tragedy, however wanting otherwise, if it has a plot, a good organization of the incidents. Further, the most interesting and emotional things in a tragedy, reversals of fortune and discoveries, are parts of the plot. It is significant that beginners in the art, like the early tragic poets, become proficient in versification, and in delineating character, before they master the construction of plots.

Mastery of plot, then, is the sign of the dramatic artist; the plot is the first principle, and, as it were, the very soul of tragedy. The tragic action is like design in painting: the most beautiful colors, laid on without order, will give less pleasure than the simplest sketch in black and white. Next in importance comes moral bent. Thought comes third. The tragic personages must speak and argue as befits a given situation, and hence the poet must

[38]

understand politics (including ethics) and the art of eloquence; thus the elder poets, as Sophocles, made their heroes speak like statesmen, while Euripides and his followers give theirs the tricks of rhetoricians. Fourth in importance comes the diction—to the modern reader it is *the* medium of poetic art; in this the poet makes his agents express their sentiments. And here Aristotle remarks that the diction is essentially the same thing whether the language is metrical or not; he anticipates Wordsworth's contention that 'there neither is, nor can be, any essential difference between the language of prose and metrical composition.' Of the other two elements, music is the more important, for it supplies the chief accessory pleasure of the drama. Sixth and last comes 'spectacle,' important as arousing our interest, but demanding a lower kind of artistic skill; indeed, it concerns the stage-manager more than the poet. A tragedy will produce its effect when read aloud, quite apart from the stage.

Aristotle now takes up in order, with a few natural digressions, the four main elements in the art of the tragic, and hence of the epic, poet, namely, plot, moral bent, thought, and

[39]

diction. Of music he says little, perhaps because of his own limitations, perhaps because poet and composer were now less closely identified than in the age of Sophocles; in any case he would probably refer the student of poetry to a technical treatise on music. Similarly he gives but incidental notice to 'spectacle,' since many matters of stage-presentation do not concern the tragic poet as such.

In dealing with plot, and the proper tragic effect, he begins with axioms that may strike the modern reader as too obvious. But Aristotle does not neglect fundamentals, as the careless may. He returns to his definition. A tragedy is an imitation of an action that is complete in itself, and has magnitude or extent; for a thing may be a whole, and yet wanting in magnitude. A whole is that which has a beginning, middle, and end. A beginning is that which does not follow anything else in a necessary sequence, but after which something else does naturally exist or come to pass. An end is that which naturally follows something else (a middle) in a necessary or usual sequence, but has nothing following it. And a middle is that which naturally follows something, and is naturally followed by something else. Here Aristotle agrees with Socrates, in the *Phædrus* of Plato, that every discourse should be a living creature, with a body of its own, and a head and feet; 'there should be a middle, beginning, and end, adapted to one another and to the whole.'

A well-constructed story, then, can not begin or end at any chance point; the poet must make the action conform to the principles just laid down. Further, the action must have magnitude, for the beauty of a work of art, like the beauty of a living organism, depends upon size as well as order. The work must be neither too small nor too great. A very minute thing will not be beautiful, for here we lose the pleasure arising from a perception of order in the parts; nor would an animal a thousand miles long, since we could not see the whole at once. (One might illustrate thus: the beauty of a snow-crystal does not appear until we magnify the object; and that of an immense crystal would escape us until we reversed the glass, and so reduced the object to dimensions we could take in at a glance.) In the same way, then, as a living creature, or an inanimate object made up of parts, must be of such magnitude that the whole and the parts may be embraced in one view, just so must the plot of a tragedy have a proper length, so that the parts and the whole may be readily embraced by the memory. And so long as the plot is perspicuous throughout, the greater the length of the story, the more beautiful will the story be—since beauty requires both magnitude and order. The time a play will consume on the stage, though a practical consideration, is only incidental to the art of tragedy. The artistic limit may be thus stated: let the length of the poem be such that the hero may fall from happiness to misery, or rise from misery to happiness, in a series of incidents linked together in a natural or inevitable sequence.

The plot must be unified. But its unity will not consist, as some suppose, in merely having one person as hero; for the experiences of the individual have no limit, and some of his deeds have no relation to others; they can not all be reduced to a unified action. Though Heracles (or Beowulf or Don Juan) is a single person, it does not follow that a story of his doings will be a unit. Homer is correct in taking some, and omitting other, incidents that are told of Odysseus, and in fitting together those that are interrelated in a causal, or at all events natural, sequence. In the *Odyssey*, as in the *Iliad*, the poet chose an action with the sort of unity here enjoined. As in painting, so in poetry, the artist must imitate a unified object. In an epic poem or tragedy, therefore, the plot must represent an action that is organically one; the arrangement of parts must be like the structure of an animal, in which the transposition or removal of a single member would make the whole look disjointed. Every part must be necessary, and in place; nothing superfluous.

The poet represents ideal, not historical, truth; not what has happened, but what is likely to happen, a sequence of events that is credible or inevitable. Herodotus tells what actually happened; turn his work into verse, and it would still be history. Metre does not make the poet. (So turning the *Odyssey* into prose does not change its nature; the poet still relates, not facts of history, but what might well happen.) Poetry is more philosophic and of a higher seriousness than history, since it tends to represent universal truth—what a typical person will say or do in a given case. Such is the aim of the poet, though he attaches actual names (Odysseus and Penelope, or Adam and Eve) to the types. Thus comic poets first construct a plot out of probable incidents, and then supply names that fit the types; as the iambic lampooners did not, for they wrongly began with invectives on the deeds of actual persons.

Yet in tragedy the poets use the names of Œdipus, Agamemnon, and others, who are said to have existed; for what we think has occurred we take to be possible—had it been impossible, it would not have occurred. In some tragedies, however, only a few of the names are familiar; and in some, both names and incidents are alike devised by the poet, who is not constrained to repeat the traditional stories; even these, familiar to but a part of the audience, may give pleasure to all.

It is clear that the poet (Greek, 'maker') is more a maker of plots than of verses; is a poet by virtue of imitating an action. Nor need he be the less a poet if he take a historical subject; for actual events may show a probable or necessary sequence, and if he represents this ideal quality in them, he is their poet.

Actions are either involved or uninvolved. Of uninvolved plots the worst are the 'episodic,' in which one incident follows another without a necessary or probable sequence; the poet either wants insight, or else pads his work so as to fill out the time on the stage. But the tragic action should be a complete whole with no irrelevant insertions.

It is also an imitation of incidents that arouse pity and fear. And such incidents are most affecting when unexpected, if one gives rise to another. An uninvolved plot has a single continuous movement; the change of fortune comes without reversal or discovery. In an involved action this change is attended by a reversal or a discovery, or by both; further, the reversal and discovery should grow out of the action itself, as the natural result of preceding events and not merely follow in point of time. In the drama, as in life, there is a vast difference between *post hoc* and *propter hoc*.

A reversal is a change from one situation to the opposite—from good fortune to bad, or from bad to good—arising in the sequence of events. Thus the Messenger comes intending to dispel Œdipus' fear that he will wed his mother, but, by disclosing his real parentage, plunges him into misery.

A discovery, or transition from ignorance to knowledge, may concern persons, things, or events, but chiefly touches persons, and thus occasions love or hate between them. Discoveries bringing love or hate, and reversals bringing happiness or misery, will excite pity or fear, the very emotions a tragedy should arouse. (So Joseph knew his brethren when they appeared in Egypt, but they did not know him. When he reveals himself, he is moved to pity, and they to fear.) Aristotle distinguishes the one-sided recognition from the case in which both sides pass from ignorance to knowledge.

Reversal and discovery are two main parts of the action. A third, 'suffering,' is an incident of a destructive or painful sort, as violent death, physical agony, or bodily wounds. (The term is not applied to mental suffering; the stabbing of Polonius, the murder of Duncan, and the suicide of Othello are true examples.)

Aristotle has now sketched the six elements or living tissues which go to form the organism, and has described the chief one, the

formative plot, in its main details. Before
analyzing these qualitative elements further,
he briefly considers the quantitative parts of
tragedy, the members, as it were, or mechanical
divisions, of the organism; he defines prologue,
episode, exode, and choric song, the last under
the sub-heads of parode, stasimon, and commos
or lament.

Then he returns to his chief interest, the
action which will produce the best tragic effect.
What should the poet aim at, and what avoid,
in forming a plot? What are the sources of the
catharsis? Let us grant that the plot should
be involved, with reversal and discovery, and
the events piteous and terrible; then three
types of story must be avoided. Good and
just men must not fall into misery, a case
neither piteous nor fearful, but revolting.
Nor must bad men be seen rising to happiness;
the situation does not even stir the human
feeling in us. Nor, again, should an exces-
sively bad man be seen falling from prosperity
into misfortune; the situation may stir some
human feeling, but not tragic pity and fear.
The bad man deserves misery in proportion;
and being bad, he is not like one of us. We
feel pity at a misfortune that outruns a man's

[47]

deserts, and fear when misfortune overtakes one like ourselves. So there remains the case of one, not superlatively good, who falls from high estate, not through vice or depravity, but through some mistake or shortcoming—a man like Œdipus (or Lear).

For perfect tragedy, then, the issue should not, as some hold, be double, fortunate for the good, unfortunate for the bad. There should be a single change of fortune, from happiness to misery, caused, not by vice or depravity, but by a serious defect in judgment or short-coming in conduct, in a person as good as the average, or better than that. Critics wrongly blame Euripides for his unhappy endings; faulty, perhaps, in other respects, he is not in this; witness the effect of these endings on the audience. The double ending, when the good triumph and the bad are worsted, as in the *Odyssey*, though preferred by some critics, is second in excellence; it is chosen by poets who yield to the wishes of the audience, and has the effect of comedy rather than tragedy proper. Pity and fear, again, may be aroused by the element of 'spectacle' (as by the dreadful masks of the Furies, or the rags of Telephus

or Lear), but should properly come from the
action and the art of the poet. The construction should be such that, away from the stage,
and without help from the eye, one who hears
the play recited will feel the chill of fear and
the stirrings of pity.

The tragic quality must be impressed upon
the incidents. When enemy offers violence to
enemy, there is nothing in his act or intention
to arouse our pity—though we pity the victim;
and similarly when the agents are neither
friends nor enemies. But when the incident
occurs within the circle of natural ties—when
murder is done or intended by brother against
brother, son against father, mother against son,
or son against mother—our pity is aroused.
The deed of horror may be done knowingly
(as in *Macbeth*), or in ignorance before the
tie is discovered. Or an irreparable injury
may be intended, and the discovery made in
time to avoid the deed; a highly emotional
situation, and in fact the best. The worst is
that in which some one, knowingly, is about
to injure a blood-relation, and then desists;
the intention is revolting, and no pity ensues
since the victim is spared. The situation is

[49]

not so bad when the victim is known, and the act performed; better yet, when the deed is done in ignorance (as Œdipus unwittingly slays his father), and the relationship afterwards discovered. Here our sense of natural affection does not revolt, and the revelation is astounding. Best of all is the case in *Iphigenia among the Taurians*, where the heroine is about to slay Orestes, and finds that he is her brother in time to save him. Since the outlines of traditional stories must be preserved, and the deed of horror treated in a preferable way, we see why tragedies have become restricted to tales of a few houses only. In searching old stories for themes, the poets more by luck than art came to embody tragic incidents in their plots; and for want of invention they still adhere to the legends of Alcmæon, Œdipus, Orestes, and other families in which deeds of horror occurred.

In depicting character, the poet should make the agents good, true to type, true to life, and self-consistent. They must lean toward goodness, and not be ineffective. As for truth to type, a woman, for example, should not possess manly valor or virile eloquence. The agents must also seem like natural human beings.

As for self-consistency, even if a changeful person is represented, his changefulness must be consistently depicted.

As the plot must show a probable or necessary relation between one incident and another, so with character: a given type must speak or act in a certain way as the necessary or natural outcome of his inner being. Then one thing will grow out of another in a necessary or probable sequence throughout, and the solution of dramatic crises will develop from the progress of the story. There will be no need of a *deus ex machina,* no call for arbitrary devices whatever unless to explain the past, outside the drama proper, or to announce events in the future—for the gods know all things. The sequence of the action proper should square with our reason; the irrational, if it can not be avoided, should lie outside the events directly presented. That Œdipus never should have learned the circumstances attending the death of his predecessor, King Laius, Aristotle regards as 'improbable'; but since they are antecedent to the tragedy, the irrational element is unnoticed.

In depicting the tragic flaw, the poet should observe the method of portrait-painters; he must preserve distinctive features like the wrath of Achilles, and yet ennoble his portrait, that of a kind and honorable man. All the foregoing principles must be observed, and such principles of stage-effect as concern the poet.

Discovery, we have seen, is a passage from ignorance to knowledge. The least artistic sort, and commonest, is recognition by signs and tokens. Yet a scar, for example, may be used in a more artistic way or a less. When the old nurse recognizes Odysseus as she comes to wash his scar, that is more artistic, and in the natural course of events; but when Odysseus bares the scar in order to prove his identity to the herdsmen, that is more forced and mechanical. Next come discoveries arbitrarily introduced by the poet, not arising from the progress of the action; as when Orestes simply reveals himself to his sister, saying not what the drama requires, but what the poet wishes. The third sort is recognition by memories; when Odysseus hears the minstrel chant the adventure of the Wooden Horse, he weeps, is observed by Alcinous, and so is identified. Fourth comes discovery by inference; in the *Libation-pourers* Electra argues: Some

[52]

one with hair like mine has come, but Orestes alone has hair like mine, therefore it is he that has come. Moreover, there is discovery by false inference. (So Joseph's brethren show Jacob the coat they had dipped in goat's blood, and Jacob says: 'It is my son's coat; an evil beast hath devoured him.') But of all discoveries the best grows out of the very nature of the incidents, as in *Œdipus Rex* an astounding revelation comes about from natural antecedents, without recourse to argument or the evidence of scars and heirlooms.

When working out his plot in diction, the poet should visualize the incidents, and assume the very attitudes and gestures of distress, anger, and the like; he will thus escape inconsistencies, and will feel and represent the emotions aright. The poetic art requires a natural plasticity, so that one may assume various personalities with ease, or else a touch of madness that will make one pass involuntarily into different states of tense emotion.

But first the poet should make an outline of the story. Aristotle shows the method with a sketch of *Iphigenia among the Taurians*, and, later, with one of the *Odyssey*. With the outline fixed, and names supplied for the agents,

[53]

one must fill in with appropriate episodes. In dramas they are short; in the epic it is they that extend the poem.

Every tragedy has a complication, leading up to the change of fortune, and an unraveling, which comprises the rest of the play. Many poets succeed better in the complication. (Shakespeare sometimes slights the unraveling.)

Through the means relied on for effect, we have four species of tragedy: the involved (like Sophocles' *Electra*), where the whole play is a recognition and reversal; that of suffering (as the *Women of Trachis*); that of character; and that of spectacle (for example, when the scene is in Hades). The poet should aim to unite all the means—or certainly the most important, and as many as possible. But the critic must take plots as the basis of judgment, comparing complication with complication, and unraveling with unraveling. The poet must show mastery in both.

Again, he must not take a multiple story like an epic for a tragedy. The story of Ilium, reduced to the scale of a drama, is disappointing; witness the ill success of those who have made the attempt. Euripides rightly takes a single phase of the story for a play.

Aristotle's contemporaries seem to have made mistakes in the art of tragedy. Yet he praises their skill in producing both involved and uninvolved plots arousing pity and fear, and the feeling we have when a bad man of great intelligence, or a brave but unjust man, is brought low. He was familiar with types resembling Shakespeare's Richard III and Macbeth. But he thinks it 'improbable' that the brave man, however unjust, will be worsted, or the clever villain outwitted. In proportion as the hero is brave and intelligent, he is apt to succeed. The reverse is probable only in Agathon's sense: 'It is likely that unlikely things will often occur.'

The chorus should be treated as a personage, an integral part of the drama, taking its share in the action. Here Sophocles is the model, and Euripides not. After Agathon the chorus sing mere interludes, unrelated to the plot, a practice much to be condemned. Every part of a drama should be organic.

From plot and character we go on to thought and diction. Thought is shown in the speeches—in the efforts of the agents to prove and refute, to arouse one another's pity, or fear, or anger, and to exaggerate or to discount the importance of things. Accordingly, the poet is referred to Aristotle's *Rhetoric* for the art of persuasion and the construction of speeches.

Finally we come to diction. In this treatise on poetry, where it properly belongs, is the earliest extant grammar, with the science of the parts of speech. Beginning with the simplest sounds (or letters), Aristotle proceeds synthetically to the point where he calls the *Iliad* one utterance through the union of more than one. He also treats of current terms, rare words, and metaphors. The poet should strive for clearness through the use of familiar terms, and for distinction through an admixture of rare words, metaphors, and other deviations from custom. (So Lincoln said, not 'Eighty-seven years ago,' but 'Four score and seven.') Most important of all is a command of metaphor. This the poet can not learn from others; it is the mark of genius, and of an insight into unapprehended similitudes.

Leaving tragedy, we turn, in the third section, to epic poetry and the principles of con-

structing it. The story should be framed on
dramatic principles, should resemble a beautiful living creature, and thus will arouse its characteristic pleasure. It should not, like history,
chronicle all that happened in a given period.
Homer avoids this common mistake. Though
the siege of Ilium has a certain unity, far from
taking all of it for his theme, he selects one
phase for his action, and subordinates other
incidents to that.

Further, the constituents of epic poetry will
be the same as in tragedy: plot, character,
thought, and diction; but tragedy has music
and spectacle besides. And again, an epic plot
must be involved or uninvolved, or the story
must be one of suffering or of character. The
Iliad has an uninvolved plot, and is a story of
tragic suffering; the *Odyssey* has an involved
plot, being full of discoveries, and is a story of
character. Both stories surpass all others in
their speeches and their diction.

But epic poetry differs from tragedy in
length and in metre. For the length, we must
be able to embrace the whole story in one view.
Perhaps the *Iliad* and *Odyssey* are somewhat
long. Yet through its capacity for extension
epic poetry has an advantage: the tragic poet

[57]

is limited to the one thing done on the stage at a given time, but the epic poet can represent simultaneous events, and thus have a wider, grander, and more diversified action.

The epic metre, the hexameter, is the fruit of experience; it is stately and impressive, and most readily admits rare words and metaphors. The iambic metre, expressing life and motion, and the trochaic, a dancing measure, are suited to the drama.

Among epic poets, Homer is the imitative artist. Others obtrude themselves into their works; he, after a brief preliminary, brings in a man or woman, distinctly characterized, to do the speaking.

The marvelous has its place in tragedy, but the irrational has more scope in the epic, where we do not see the action. On the stage, the pursuit of Hector by Achilles would be ridiculous; in the narrative, the absurdity of the situation is not observed.

Our delight in the marvelous is shown in the details men add when repeating a story. But Homer knows how a lie should be told. Without dwelling on the main statement, a poet should elaborate details which would follow if that were true, as Homer makes Odysseus do in lying to Penelope.

A sequence of events which looks reasonable, though actually impossible, should be preferred by the poet to what, though really possible, seems incredible. In any case the irrational element should lie outside the story proper. It is silly to urge that we should ruin the work by omitting such things; the poet is free to choose his theme and to construct aright. But he may treat improbabilities less artistically, or more so—as Homer conceals them in the *Odyssey* by artistic elaboration.

The last section of the *Poetics* contains a solution of critical problems, and a defence of Homer.

The solutions rest on the principles of imitation. The poet, being an imitator, must represent things as they were or are, as they are said or thought to be, or as they ought to be. Again, his medium is the diction, either unadorned, or with such admixture of rare words and metaphors as we concede to poets. And again, poetry has its own standard of correctness; thus we must not judge the conduct of Achilles by ethical standards. A poet is in danger of committing two sorts of error: wrong choice of subject, and wrong treatment of it. If, choosing wrongly, he yet succeeds in his imitation, the fault does not concern his art, though of course he should not make *any* mistakes.

Representing an impossibility is a fault, to be condoned, however, if an artistic purpose is subserved; thus the pursuit of Hector serves to astound us. But when scientific accuracy answers as well, the fault is not justified.

If the poet seems untrue to fact, our reply may be that he has represented the typical; according to Sophocles, he himself drew men as they ought to be, Euripides men as they are. If there seems to be truth neither to fact nor ideal, the poet may yet be in accord with current legends and assertions; unedifying tales of the gods may be untrue, but if people believe them, Homer may accept them. Or again, an alleged fact, not now true, may have been so in his time.

As for acts and utterances in the story, we must consider not merely their intrinsic nobility or baseness, but who says or does the thing, to whom it is said or done, or when, or for whom, or with what motive. Other criticisms must be tested by the principles of poetic diction. A rare word may look like a common one with another meaning; or we may interpret a poetic metaphor too literally, or think a passage incorrect when in fact we have wrongly pronounced or punctuated it. Then there are possible ambiguities in grammar, and differences in usage at different times. If a word has more than one meaning, we must ascertain the poet's sense before condemning him.

We must not prejudge, but, as Glaucon suggests, first scrutinize our premises. If the poet seems to contradict himself, we should test him by the method of sophistical refutations, with customary good sense as the standard. The critic is justified in censuring improbability in the action, when the irrational serves no artistic purpose, and depravity in the agents, when the plot does not require it.

Last of all comes the problem: Which is the higher form, epic poetry, or tragedy? Is epic poetry addressed to the better audience, and tragedy a vulgar pantomimic art for the crowd, in which the actors play the ape and contort their bodies? Gestures, we may reply, belong to the interpreter, not the poet, and

[61]

may be overdone in reciting epic poetry, too. Nor is all bodily movement to be condemned —otherwise we condemn all choral dancing; it is ignoble attitudes and gestures that are to be censured. Besides, tragedy has its effect, like epic poetry, when merely read aloud.

Then, to the four elements of epic poetry tragedy adds spectacle and music, and through the music its effect is heightened, while its greater vividness is felt off the stage as well as on. And it attains its end in less space: the concentrated effect is the more delightful. Again, we find a stricter unity of action in the tragic than in the epic poets, though the *Iliad* and the *Odyssey* are as nearly perfect as epic poetry can be.

We conclude that tragedy is the higher form: it fulfils its purpose better; for we recall that the two forms are to give us, not any chance pleasure, but the catharsis of pity and fear.

III. THE POETICS ILLUSTRATED FROM GENESIS

THE foregoing abstract gains interest when we test it by the Biblical story of Joseph (Gen. 37, 39–45).

The author takes a story which is the more credible because we believe that the incidents once occurred; and history does now and then evince the universal quality that the poet must secure. The story has all the marks of an epic poem save length and metre; and metre is not the essential thing. The one essential is artistic imitation.

This story is an artistic imitation, in embellished language, of an action that is serious, complete, and of such length that the hero may pass from misery into great good fortune; the incidents are linked together in a natural sequence. The action, while not strictly involved, is yet full of discoveries and reversals; and the story is one of character. Joseph, a man like ourselves, or better, errs in flaunting his youthful dreams of superiority, and angers his brethren as a tell-tale; but his flaw is not

[63]

tragic, and hence the issue, as in the *Odyssey*, is rather that of comedy. For a man so good and just as he, a miserable end would be revolting. Yet pity and fear are aroused, and in the right way, by some of the incidents.

The general outline is this: A certain youth, beloved of his father, is hated by his brothers, who intend to slay him, yet through the favor of one it chances that he is sold as a slave into a far country, where he is cast into prison. At length, through his interpretation of dreams, he gains favor with the king of that land, rises to high estate, and saves his father and brothers from famine. The rest is in the nature of episode.

But the episodes are suitable. Thus it is probable that one of his brothers should wish to save him, that Potiphar's wife should spitefully betray him, and that in a land of magicians his interpretation of dreams should deliver him from prison.

The chief persons in the story are mostly good; and all are true to type, true to life, and self-consistent. So Jacob is a typical doting father, speaks and acts as old men do in life, and is consistently portrayed; and Pharaoh is the Oriental monarch, peremptory and fatal, sometimes indulgent, sometimes harsh; his inconsistency with the butler and baker is consistently portrayed, and true to life. Joseph is good and efficient, first a typical youth, and then a typical ruler, true to life in dealing with his brothers and men in general, and throughout self-consistent.

There is a natural, often necessary, relation between his character and his acts, utterances, and sufferings. As a favorite son he naturally aroused envy in his brothers. As the youngest, and the son of a favored wife, he was dear to his aging father, and likely to be championed by his eldest brother. A virtuous young man and trusted overseer, he repelled the advances of his master's wife. And as a Hebrew he displayed poetic vision and business foresight, and so obtained for Pharaoh a monopoly of the grain; thus he brought all the arable land of Egypt into the possession of the Crown.

The three parts of a plot, suffering, discovery, and reversal, grow naturally out of antecedent events. Physical suffering occurs when Joseph is stripped and cast into the pit, when he is imprisoned in Egypt, and when the chief baker is hanged. The story is full of discoveries. The youth seeks his brethren, and they see him afar off and conspire against him. Reuben, returning to the pit, discovers that Joseph is gone. The brethren dip the coat in blood, and Jacob falsely infers that Joseph is slain. The author delights in representing false inferences. With Joseph's garment, the wicked wife convinces Potiphar that the young man had made the advances; and as ruler of Egypt Joseph himself guilefully causes false discoveries when the purchase-money, secretly returned, is found in the grain-sacks. We note also Joseph's recognition of the brethren when first they appear in Egypt, and he barely escapes being discovered, 'through memories,' by retiring in order that they may not see him weep; the actual discovery when he makes himself known; the mutual recognition between Joseph and Jacob, and the meeting between Jacob and Pharaoh. When the dreams of Joseph, the chief butler and baker, and Pharaoh come true, we have discovery of a general sort. Discovery is also attended by reversal of fortune. When the brothers see Joseph in the field, they cast him into the pit, and then sell him. He rises to fortune in the house of Potiphar only to fall into prison. Here again he wins favor, though at the lowest ebb of his fortunes. At length he is released, and rises to great prosperity at the court of Pharaoh. Jacob suffers a reversal in the loss of Joseph, in the famine, and in the detention of his sons in Egypt; and again, they and Joseph are restored to him, and he is entertained by Pharaoh. The author shows skill in the duplex reversal for the butler and baker, with the ironical joke about the *lifting up of heads*.

Though the tale ends happily, the deed of horror within the family is well handled. The intended violence of the brethren against Joseph arouses our fear, yet the outcome is not revolting; nevertheless the hero suffers, and we pity him. Pity and fear are likewise stirred by the anguish of the aged father, whose favoritism has its natural result in the vengeance of the brethren, while the distress of the old man is out of proportion to his fault.

Thought is shown in both speech and act: 'Come now therefore, and let us slay him, and cast him into the pit, and we will say: "Some evil beast hath devoured him." And we shall see what will become of his dreams.' Or again we observe it in Joseph's interpretations.

A narrative tolerates, better than a drama, the introduction of marvels. These are further justified by the character of Joseph, who is given to dreaming, by the removal of the scene to Egypt, by the antiquity of the tale, and by popular belief: So it was in the olden time, and so people say. Moreover, the outcome of the dreams astounds us.

The diction is clear without being mean. Current terms make it clear, and archaic forms lend distinction: 'And Joseph dreamed a dream, and he told it to his brethren; and they hated him yet the more.' The dreams, too, have the nature of metaphor or similitude. The author had an eye for resemblances that escape the ordinary mind.

As a Biblical writer, he might be considered an enthusiast; but he is also a plastic genius, and readily 'imitates' one personage after another, a Jacob, a Joseph, a Reuben, a keeper of a prison, a Pharaoh. Nor does he intrude himself into the story. After a brief preliminary, he introduces a clearly-marked type, dramatically conceived and alive. His imitation of an action is artistic in plot, character, thought, and diction—in all the elements of a dramatic story.

[68]

IV. AN ARISTOTELIAN
TREATMENT OF
COMEDY

THE *Poetics*, we saw, does not keep its promise regarding comedy. Did Aristotle ever discuss this? It is only reasonable to think so; yet if his analysis has come down in tangible shape, it must be in the scheme or fragment known as the *Tractatus Coislinianus*,[4] which in part is concerned with Aristophanes. The Tractate is a strange and puzzling abstract. Nevertheless some parts of it at least betray the workings of a master-mind. Its three pages or less of Greek are worth more in the interpretation of comedy than all modern essays on comedy together.

After noting the place of comedy among the types of poetic art, it begins with a definition echoing that of tragedy in the *Poetics*: 'Comedy is an imitation of an action that is ludicrous and defective, of adequate magnitude; [in language variously embellished,] the several kinds of embellishment being severally used in different parts of the play; carried on by agents, not in the form of narrative; through pleasure and laughter effecting a catharsis of the comic emotions. Comedy has laughter for its mother.'

Laughter arises from the language used, or from the objects themselves (things, persons, thoughts, and deeds). Under diction we have seven heads: First, homonyms. (Words identical in sound, but with different meanings. Tramp says to tourist: 'Speaking of bathing in famous springs, I bathed in the spring of '86.') Secondly, synonyms. (Different names for the same concept. ' "Convey" the wise it call. "Steal," foh! a fico for the phrase!' [5]) Thirdly, garrulity. (This means idle prating, long-winded folly of every sort. Shakespeare's Dogberry is garrulous in the pompous style.) Fourthly, paronyms, formed by addition or clipping. (So, by addition, Gadshill's 'long-staff sixpenny strikers,' and 'mad mustachio purple-hued malt-worms.') Fifthly, diminutives. ('Coinlet' for 'coin,' and 'gibelet' for 'gibe' in Aristophanes' *Babylonians*.[6]) Sixthly, perverting words by voice or the sense of them by gesture. (Touchstone: 'I am here with thee and thy goats, as the most capricious poet, honest Ovid, was among the

Goths'—a play on Latin *caper,* 'goat,' with perversion of 'Goths' into *goats.*) Seventhly, grammar. (Ludicrous syntax and the like. Launce: 'I'll but lean, and my staff understands me.' Speed: 'It stands under thee, indeed.')

Under laughter from the objects we have nine heads. (It is hard to dissociate a thing from its name; but if the humor disappears when the language is altered, the laughter arises from the diction, and if not, then from the objects.) Under the objects, first comes assimilation of the worse to the better, and vice versa. (Bottom is assimilated to a donkey, while Aristophanes calls Brasidas and Cleon the 'pestle' and 'mortar' of Sparta and Athens; a time-honored comic device is the substitution of servants for masters.) Secondly, deception. (In a sense, all laughter arises from cheated expectation. In the *Frogs* we expect Dionysus to bring Euripides back from Hades—and he brings Æschylus instead.) Thirdly, the impossible. ('It is easier for a camel to go through the eye of a needle than for a rich man to enter into the kingdom of God'; 'Woe unto you, scribes and pharisees, . . . which strain at a gnat, and swallow a camel.') Fourthly, the possible and inconsequent. (Dionysus' test of poetry by weighing verses of Æschylus and Euripides in scales.) Fifthly, the unexpected. (So the refusal of the corpse in the *Frogs*, to carry the luggage: 'Strike me alive if I do!') Sixthly, debasing the personages. (As with Dogberry and Falstaff.) Seventhly, ridiculous dancing. (See the witch-dance in *Tam o' Shanter*.) Eighthly, having the choice of fine things, and taking worthless. (When asked if he will hear fairy music, Bottom says: 'I have a reasonable good ear in music; let us have the tongs and the bones.') Ninthly, when the story is disjointed and without sequence. (Dogberry: 'Secondarily, they are slanders; sixth and lastly, they have belied a lady; thirdly, they have verified unjust things.')

The lampooner openly censures the evil in men; comedy uses 'emphasis.' Yet the comic poet makes both physical and mental shortcomings ridiculous.

As in tragedy there should be a due proportion of fear, so in comedy a due proportion of laughter. (This may mean that the ridiculous element should be balanced by the beautiful music—as in *The Tempest*.)

The Tractate notes the same constituents of comedy that the *Poetics* gives for tragedy: plot, character, thought, diction, music, and spectacle. Comic characters are the buffoonish (as Falstaff), the ironical (as the Platonic Socrates), and those of the impostors (quacks, pettifoggers, Tartuffe, and so on).

The parts of thought are opinion and proof. (Feste: 'What is the opinion of Pythagoras concerning wild-fowl?' Malvolio: 'That the soul of our grandam might haply inhabit a bird.') Proofs (persuasions) are of five sorts. First, Oaths. (See Molière's *'Juro'* in *Le Malade Imaginaire.*) Secondly, compacts (as that between Falstaff and the Prince to rob the travelers). Thirdly, testimonies (as Dogberry's 'O that he were here to write me down an ass'). Fourthly, ordeals (as the test of the candidate in *Le Malade Imaginaire*). Fifthly, laws. (In *Les Femmes Savantes* the cook is discharged for breaking the laws of grammar.)

The diction of comedy is the popular idiom, but the poet must make an alien speak as such. (Molière in general writes limpid French, but his domestics speak in dialect.) For the element of music the poet must consult technical treatises. After alluding to the

[73]

utility of spectacle, the Tractate goes on to the quantitative parts of comedy: prologue, choricon, episode, and exode. It ends by differentiating Old, New, and Middle Comedy. (In Shakespeare, the Falstaff-episodes are of the 'old' type, *The Comedy of Errors* is of the 'new,' and *The Tempest* is intermediate.)

In our limited space one could only hint at a few of the ways in which the Tractate throws light upon both ancient and modern comedy. The fragment belongs to the Peripatetic tradition; I incline to share the belief of English scholars, as opposed to German, that in essentials it represents some part of Aristotle's work on poetry.

V. MAIN TENETS OF ARISTOTLE
REGARDING POETRY

FOR modern readers a difficult postulate of
Aristotle is that of *imitation*. To us the word
suggests a servile copy; we think ill of an
artist who is not 'original': the poet should
look at things for himself, and express them
in his own way. A like objection is brought
against imitative art by the Socrates of Plato's
Ion and *Republic:* ideas, the true realities,
exist in the mind of God alone; even visible
objects are imperfect copies of the truth; and
the artist imitates these imperfect copies in a
false semblance of a bed or table, so that his
work is at two removes from the true idea.
With Aristotle, the artist does look at reality;
life is the very thing the poet represents. The
painter imitates, not a particular bed or table,
but the true idea thereof. 'I have at all times
endeavored to look steadily at my subject,'
said Wordsworth; [7] he steadily contemplated
men in action, and thus imitated universal
forms. Aristotle may have no term for our

'creative imagination,' but his concept implies an artistic activity amounting to creative vision.

The result of this activity is something vital. A work of art is like a living organism. The thought is not peculiar to Aristotle, having already occurred to Plato, and indeed is basic in any fruitful theory of art. The poet is like the Creator in giving to a work of art the organic quality we find in the works of nature. And art completes nature. Omitting the accidental or superfluous, the artist seeks the end toward which nature is striving, and completes the effort in a rounded whole. The artist, however, represents the idea in a medium chosen by himself. The animal is one thing, its representation in words or pigments another. This organic comparison is perhaps more consistently worked out in the *Poetics* than in any other critical treatise we know. It appears even in chance-allusions. When dwelling on the need of structure in a poem, Aristotle will compare a disjointed work of art to an animal that has suffered a painful and striking dislocation of a limb.

The structure of the whole is vital, the medium in which the artist works less important. Whether one chooses metrical language, or merely writes in prose, is of no great significance. The question is, does the writer use his imagination? Does he represent men engaged in a great and unified action, with its parts duly fitted together? English has no accepted term for the literary artist in imaginative prose, as Aristotle found no Greek word embracing prose dramas and imaginary dialogues. German, however, uses *dichtung* for poetical or imaginative composition whether in verse or prose.

The characteristic of poetry being the typical representation of men in action, Aristotle insists on the 'probability' of that action. Does the poet represent what may or, better, must occur, given the agents and the initial situation? What follows must not merely be possible. Possibly a clever villain like Richard III, or a brave wrong-doer like Macbeth, will be outwitted or worsted; but intelligence and courage are likely to succeed, and hence the failure of such persons is not typical, being neither probable nor necessary. The artist may render it more plausible through a sequence of events, but the initial situation is not promising. Probability in the sequence, is, of course, the poet's major concern, according to Aristotle. Nowadays we think of probability and possibility in a vague way as related to things in general. Aristotle mainly thinks of a consequent as probable or necessary in relation to definite antecedents. Before you may have a dramatic incident B, you must have an A from which it naturally or inevitably springs, and so on throughout the play.

Thus the hero falls as the natural outcome of an ethical flaw or some grave misjudgment in a crisis—of his tragic *hamartia*. The word, borrowed from archery, later appears as the New Testament equivalent for 'sin.' Lear misses the mark through his 'hideous rashness' in dividing his kingdom and misjudging the loyal Cordelia. Fierce and obstinate wrath in Achilles, with Agamemnon's error in seizing the girl Briseis, brings on all the woes of the *Iliad*. The point is illustrated in all great tragic stories; Saintsbury [8] thinks Aristotle's insistence on it his chief contribution to critical theory. But it may have been noted by Greek critics in treatises that are lost, for the *hamartia* is a matter of conscious art in the poets, as in Sophocles' delineation of Œdipus or of

[78]

Creon, the hero in *Antigone*. In comedy, too,
there should be a necessary or probable relation between comic flaws or foibles and the
incidents of the action; we may infer this
from the *Poetics,* and may illustrate with
Molière's Miser and Hypochondriac.

But Aristotle's great contribution to the
study of literature lies in his perspective, as
shown in the demand that each kind of art
shall produce its own effect. Everything else
is subordinate; the final aim determines all.
Without organic unity, there is no art, and
hence no pleasure; without the tragic flaw in
a noble nature, you can not move an audience
to fear and pity, the relief of which is the
end of tragedy; without embellishments, you
can hardly make a painful story pleasing.
Again, this pleasure is bound up with our delight in learning, characteristic of men as men,
and to be distinguished from animal satisfac-
tions. Hence springs our pleasure in the
artistic imitation as a whole, when we learn
the outcome of the play; hence also our
pleasure in details such as recognitions and
reversals, when the unknown is seen to be
the heroine's brother, or the sudden turn of
fortune a result of previous events. And the

[79]

aim of the poet *is* pleasure, not the arousal of pity and fear—that is only the means; the all-important end is tragic delight.

The *Poetics* contains the beginnings of scientific grammar. The fact is significant, though some readers are puzzled by the attention given to this topic in such a work. But grammar had to be treated in connection either with rhetoric or the art of poetry; so far as we know, there was no systematic treatment of it in existence; and the subject is fundamental in literary art. The imperfections of Aristotle's grammar may be forgiven in a pioneer; his principles are better than those of the Latin grammarians, by which the modern study is dominated.

So much for positive values. On the negative side we are provided against common misapprehensions in criticism. First, we learn that the standard of conduct is not the same in imitative art as in ethics or politics. A character in fiction should not be needlessly bad; an Edmund, a Regan, a Goneril must be considered, not ethically, but artistically wrong, if they are worse than the action requires. Nor may we judge the utterances of fictitious personages as if they were made in real life, or belonged to the author .himself. It is a mistake to attribute to Milton the sentiments of his Satan, a debased Stoic, a liar, and a master of sophistry, a character so well depicted as to dupe the reader himself; Satan's rhetoric, according to the poet, has 'semblance of worth, not substance.' The half-truth, 'Fallen cherub, to be weak is miserable,' uttered in agonized bravado, is not the sentiment of Milton, who agreed with Paul: 'When I am weak, then am I strong.' Similarly, the maxims of a senile Polonius are not to be taken for the native wisdom of Shakespeare. Giving heed to the *Poetics* will save us from such mistakes.

It should keep us, too, from recognizing but one sort of poetic temperament. Aristotle properly distinguishes between the plastic type and the enthusiastic. The plastic Sophocles or Shakespeare readily assumes rôle after rôle, until we are tempted to ask whether he has a fixed personality of his own; the innermost core of Chaucer eludes us. The enthusiastic poet, an Æschylus, a Dante, a Milton, is in himself a man of intense feelings, though his power may be so ruled by art that he will construct very suitable agents for his plot.

[81]

The distinction is one of tendencies, and a given poet may share in both. Milton and Wordsworth are rather of the enthusiastic type, yet they, like the Biblical writers, have more of the plastic quality than most readers observe. And a great plastic dramatist like Sophocles must be convincing: if he throws himself into one personality after another, there must be a self that he can project.

Before leaving Aristotle's main ideas, we may consider two aspects of tragedy with which some say the *Poetics* has failed to reckon. One is the aspect of struggle—the conflict between a hero and external 'forces,' or between him and his 'fate.' But the notion of a tragic struggle is implicit in the terms of the *Poetics*. Thus, in describing what the persons of tragedy do and suffer, Aristotle uses the verb *dran*, the strongest possible word. He rightly conceives of the drama, not as a struggle between a man and a 'force'; the objects of imitation, he insists, are 'men in action.' If one man meditates injuring another, a struggle is likely to result.

Secondly, there is the notion of 'fate,' supposedly a controlling motive in the ancient drama. There is, however, but one agency against which a Greek hero may not hope to contend—and that is the poet. Sophocles, not destiny, controls the action; having planned a tragic outcome, he makes Œdipus take the wrong course at every juncture. Aristotle says enough about the inevitable sequence of a well-constructed play; if he neglects the workings of 'fate,' the reason is that they are less important in Greek tragedy than our writers imagine. An arbitrary fate is 'irrational,' and the sort of thing he would exclude from the action. But it is 'probable' that a tragic hero will talk of destiny in excusing his own blindness of heart. Sophocles makes Œdipus and Creon attribute their faulty choices sometimes to fate, and again to folly. Such utterances proceed, not from the clear-eyed Sophocles, but from characters represented by him as likely to err. Iocasta, a fatalist, scouts the oracles, and then hangs herself. University students, when asked how Antigone comes to die, will say, 'Through force of circumstances.' But she, too, is a suicide. She would have been rescued from the tomb had she been less fatalistic, and as 'ready at need' as Odysseus in the cave of the Cyclops.

VI.   COMPOSITION AND STYLE
OF THE POETICS

THE *Poetics* no doubt came into being after
Aristotle settled as teacher and investigator
at Athens in 335 B.C., and before he left
Athens in 323. It may have been written
after both the *Rhetoric* and the *Politics*. But
almost nothing can be safely stated regarding
the chronological order of his works. He
taught virtually the entire circle of learning,
and must have given the parts in rotation,
so that his memoranda for different courses
would exist side by side over a period of years,
undergoing occasional revision as his knowledge and views matured. The *Poetics* shows
the author in the fulness of his powers. True,
it has crabbed passages arising from haste
as well as concision; and there may be inter-
polation, though not so much as scholars once
supposed. Then his rapid Greek mind will
let the Stagirite glide over inconsistencies, and
now and then force an illustration to suit a
principle. But he is no sophist, nor given

to the study of words rather than substance. Very fond of logic, and tending perhaps to judge a poem too exclusively by formulas, he has a great, simple, normal mind, demanding that, whatever poetry may contain, it must be founded in good sense. If he makes less of the supra-rational element than the august figures of the gods in Homer, Æschylus, and Sophocles deserve, he still finds some place in his theory for the marvelous, for the 'enthusiastic' poet, and for those deities who know all things. In the extremely concise *Poetics* the number of lucid and even eloquent passages is noteworthy. We find even touches of dry humor, as in the example of a beast a thousand miles long.

In fact, the style is admirably suited to the matter. Aristotle, no rhapsode in criticism, does not, like Shelley or Ruskin, attempt poetic flights in a scientific treatise on art, but is more like Leonardo in his treatise on painting, and Burke *On the Sublime and Beautiful*. Leonardo could produce beautiful paintings, and Burke noble orations; like them, Aristotle knows how to write unadorned prose in dealing with a scientific topic.

[85]

VII. THE POETICS IN ANTIQUITY

THE after-history of the *Poetics* in antiquity
is obscure, and its influence at Alexandria, and
down to the Roman poets, orators, and critics,
or later, can not be disentangled from that
of Greek critical writings, some by Aristotle,
that are lost. Aristotle's criticism must have
been useful to his friend Theodectes and other
dramatists of the same generation, and have
gained currency through Theophrastus, his
friend and pupil, and successor as head of
their school. Theophrastus himself wrote on
tragedy and comedy, and had as pupil Men-
ander, who while a stripling, before he ex-
hibited comedies, may have talked with Aristotle. Another poet of the New Comedy,
Philemon, had been exhibiting plays several
years before Aristotle left Athens, and was
likely to know the philosopher and current
theories of art. But did Aristotle's eminence
make his theory stand out superior among
contemporary works of the sort? And did
he actually write on comedy, and pass the

tradition on to Theophrastus? Does the *Tractatus Coislinianus* go back to him or to Theophrastus, or to some later critic who possessed a body of Greek critical writings from Aristotle down? Only the discovery of manuscripts could lead to a certain answer. The Roman Cicero had no good knowledge of the *Poetics;* he seems to offer us a little more on the Greek theory of comedy than of tragedy; yet Aristotle's writings were published at Rome by Cicero's contemporary, Andronicus of Rhodes. Quintilian offers less than Cicero; the practical Romans were more interested in Aristotle's *Rhetoric* than in theories of poetry. But what of the Roman poets? The epic of Virgil is the offspring of Alexandrian learning, yet in certain ways runs counter to Aristotle's chief demands, and at most owes an indirect debt to the *Poetics.* Virgil did not learn the principles of construction from the Alexandrian commentators to the extent that Milton later did from those of Italy.

With Horace the case is different. The *Ars Poetica* is obviously related to the treatise of Aristotle, and yet the relation is hard to define. Horace writes a versified letter, not a scientific tract. The customary title, *Ars*

Poetica, first appears in Quintilian. In the collected works of Horace, this letter to the Pisos follows the other *Epistles,* and resembles them, as it and they follow the *Satires,* and share in the nature of satire. The satirical tinge in the *Ars Poetica* is frequently missed. Yet the *Epistles* are less satirical than the *Satires,* and the *Ars Poetica* less epistolary than the *Epistles.* In its day treatises of every sort took the shape of letters; most of the New Testament, with its varied content, appears in this form. So the essay *On the Sublime,* ascribed to Longinus, but doubtless of the first century A. D., is ostensibly a letter.

The *Ars Poetica,* then, is an epistle, lively, sensible, epigrammatic, addressed to a friend and his two sons, the elder of whom needed critical warning more than encouragement. Horace wished to please and instruct them as much by his terse and sparkling lines as by the good sense embalmed in his polished maxims. With the air of unstudied chat, the substance nevertheless has a fairly settled order—and yet no organized plan, like Aristotle's, with subordination of the less important matters. There is no deep perspective; ideas of unequal weight follow one another in an easy association on a bright flat surface. Horace may never have studied the *Poetics*, yet he surely recognized some of his doctrines as Aristotelian. But he certainly read Plato; he mingles drafts from the Dialogues with the thought of Aristotle as interpreted at Alexandria. One Neoptolemus of Parium having embodied notable matters from Aristotle in a Greek versified treatise, Horace may be following this, or a similar source, for his main ideas, and even in style, apart from his own felicitous banter. His clear-cut maxims also reflect personal observation of men and poetry; they are generalizations, not platitudes.

Aristotle, unlike Horace, says little of genius, and nothing on the need of it in the would-be poet, on the conjoint offices of nature and art, or on polishing one's verses and long withholding them from publication. Of these Alexandrian commonplaces, one may have been known to Horace in the Greek lines formerly ascribed to Simylus, a poet of the Middle Comedy: 'Nature without art will not suffice for any work, nor yet will art suffice if natural gifts be wanting.' The stress of Horace on the mechanics of verse, on the dual function of poetry in profit and delight, and on propriety and variety of style, does not savor of Aristotle's *Poetics*. But the sound remarks on organic unity, dramatic action, the evolution of the plot, the consistent presentation of character, and the emotional effect of tragedy, are Aristotelian; and similarly the high place assigned to the successful dramatist. The observations on comedy supplement the *Poetics,* but as they deal with Roman adaptations of the New Greek Comedy, and as Horace on the Old Greek Comedy is stereotyped and vague, he does not reflect the substance of the *Tractatus Coislinianus.*

The latter tradition survives in the scholiasts on Aristophanes, who also ineptly utilize terms from Aristotle's *Rhetoric;* while the tradition of our *Poetics* is a trickling in the sand of scholiasts and grammarians in general. We have small means of following it in the Græco-Roman world after the time of Horace. Vestiges of Aristotelian theory in Strabo (64 B. C.– A. D. C. 21) are seen in his excellent criticism of Homer as poet and geographer; Strabo shares the view that poetry should teach as well as please, yet he is closer to the *Poetics* than is Horace. Somewhat later, the concept

of imitation is misunderstood by Plutarch
(A. D. c. 46–c. 120), in whose time the principles of Aristotle seem to have been distorted
by intermediate compends and text-books.

VIII. THE POETICS IN THE MIDDLE AGES

In the fourth-century Latin grammarians, a popular definition of tragedy, ascribed to Theophrastus, but perhaps originally in Aristotle's dialogue *On Poets,* has replaced the technical definition of the *Poetics.* This popular notion found in Diomedes and Donatus prevailed throughout the Middle Ages. Thus Dante unites the ideas of tragedy and comedy in the grammarians with Horatian precepts, adding flavor with a borrowed allusion to the Senecan tragedies, which it seems he had not read. In mediæval writers the distinction between narrative poetry and dramatic is hardly felt. The usual conception appears in a gloss by Chaucer on his translation of Boethius: 'Tragedy is to seyn a dite of a prosperity for a time that endeth in wrecchidnesse.' It is amplified in the Monk's Prologue:

> Tragedie is to seyn a certain storie,
> As olde bookes maken us memorie,
> Of him that stood in great prosperitie,

And is yfallen out of heigh degree
Into myserie, and endeth wrecchedly.
And they ben versified communely
Of six feet, which men clepen exametron.
In prose eek been endyted many oon,
And eek in metre, in many a sondry wyse.

The hero is of high estate; the play or tale begins in calm; then suddenly comes irreparable harm. The mediæval notion survives well into the Renaissance, underlying, for example, much of the Elizabethan drama. Indeed, it still survives in the popular usage by which sheer accident or brutal murder is called a 'tragedy.'

For Western Europe in the earlier Middle Ages there is no history of the *Poetics*. Shreds of Aristotle's thought may have drifted down, unrecognized, along with the *Ars Poetica*, which contains Aristotelian doctrines in popular form, and was later the one important ancient critical treatise read by Dante. Even in the Renaissance, and almost to our own times, the lively epistle of Horace has had better success than the Greek treatise with readers in general. But when the *Poetics* again became known, and was studied in Italy, the technical conception of tragedy crept in, made headway, then existed side by side with the mediæval definition, sometimes in the same Renaissance author, and finally replaced it in critical treatises. However, we must not anticipate.

For a while, then, we lose sight of the treatise in Europe. Was it occasionally studied? We might infer so from the existence of manuscripts; if unknown scribes labored at copying the work, it must have had a value for some one. But even regarding this meagre evidence there is a gap in our knowledge between the fifth century and the ninth. In Europe the interval is a blank.

Not so perhaps in Syria and Arabia, where Greek learning continued, and even flourished, after its decline at Alexandria and Rome. In the fifth century the philosophy of Aristotle was known among the Syrians of Edessa; in the sixth, works of his were translated into Syriac by Sergius of Resaina. The Syrians and Arabians were interested in Greek logic and medicine; but we need not infer that they neglected the *Poetics*. Alpharabius at Bagdad and Damascus, about the end of the ninth century, seems to have known the *Rhetoric;*

the two works were then likely to be together. About the same time a Nestorian monk, perhaps at Edessa, verbally translated the *Poetics* into Syriac, from a more complete and accurate Greek manuscript than any we now possess, one dating from the fifth or sixth century at the latest, and evidently supplied with marginal notes, but ending where our manuscripts do.[9] Of this Syriac version only a single page remains. But the whole in its time was translated into Arabic by Abu'l Bashar Mattā (990–1037), whose work is extant in a mutilated eleventh-century manuscript at Paris. On the misleading Arabic text, again, was based the short paraphrase by the Arabian philosopher Averroes (1126–1198), a native of Cordova. To him the *Poetics,* at three removes from the original, is a hopeless enigma; he neither comprehends the sense of the treatise nor knows anything of the masterpieces to which it refers.

Through the Mohammedan conquest, Arabic learning spread westward, and in Spain we return to the European history of the *Poetics.* The manuscript used by the Syrian translator was perhaps 500 years earlier than the oldest now extant, which may be dated about the

year 1000; both doubtless were Byzantine.
At the wanderings of the Arabic version we
can only guess. The abridgment by Averroes
was translated into Hebrew, Arabic learning
in Spain being largely Jewish. It was also
translated into Latin by Hermannus Aleman-
nus at Toledo in 1256 with the title *Aristotelis
Poetria*. The *Rhetoric* he put into Latin from
the Arabic version entire, but for the *Poetics*
he attempted only the commentary of Averroes, he says, because of the differences between
Greek and Arabic metres (!), because of ob-
scurity in the wording, and 'for several other
reasons.' Roger Bacon (c. 1214–1294) consulted Hermann's *Aristotelis Poetria*, but not
the Greek *Poetics*, nor any Latin translation
from the Greek; the reference in Part Four
of Bacon's *Opus Majus* is the first by any
Englishman to Aristotle's treatise. Like Al-
farabi, he includes rhetoric and poetic as parts
of logic; he is here concerned with mathematics
as related to persuasion, and with Aristotle's
book *'de poetico argumento'* through an interest in the embellishments of prose, metre, and
rhythm. Hermann could not disclose to Bacon
the nature of the *Poetics*.

If, then, the foremost English scholar of

his day, who read both Arabic and Hebrew, and was zealous for the study of Greek, knew the treatise only in this roundabout and sorry fashion, his Western contemporaries outside of Spain are unlikely to have been more fortunate. Dante shows no acquaintance with it in any shape, though the *Politics, Ethics,* and *Rhetoric*—in fact, most of Aristotle's other writings—were, through Arabic and Jewish scholarship in Spain, through the paraphrases of Albertus Magnus and the commentaries of Aquinas, and through the Dominicans annually sent to Greece to learn the language, fairly well understood on the Continent before the *Divina Commedia* was written. There was a Latin translation of the *Rhetoric* from the Greek, but not of the *Poetics*. The fourth Crusade (1202–4) established relations between Italy and Constantinople; but if by chance Byzantine scholars latterly had studied the *Poetics,* that made no difference to the rest of Europe. Their acquaintance with the work did not extend to familiarity; they read Greek tragedy, but in the light of a pedantic grammar and rhetoric. The Constantinopolitan John Tzetzes (c. 1110–c. 1180 or 1185) wrote in puerile verse on tragic poetry; [10] his stray hints of Aristotle betoken no real debt to the *Poetics*. And yet between the fourth Crusade and the Fall of Constantinople in 1453, Greek manuscripts of the *Poetics*, and Greeks who could read them, must have gone to Italy.

There is no other explanation of the fact that Italian scholars studied the work in the second half of the fifteenth century—unless we assume that the Byzantine scholars all waited until the Turks gave the last stroke to the Eastern Empire, and then took flight in a body to the Italian universities. Their flight, and the transfer of manuscripts, were doubtless intermittent, with frequent accelerations. It is said that in the hundred years before 1453 the Turks crossed the Bosphorus twenty times.

IX. THE POETICS IN THE RENAISSANCE—ITALY

Although the modern study of the *Poetics* is often dated from the latter half of the fifteenth century, the beginnings really are hidden. No doubt Hermann's Latin version of Averroes had reached Italy as well as the England of Roger Bacon; but there was another Latin translation, by Martinus of Tortosa, Spain, in the fourteenth century. And Averroes' teachings, taken over from the Jews, were current at the University of Padua in the time of Luther; the Latin abridgment of the *Poetics* was printed at Venice in 1481, and again in 1525. The Arabic subordination of poetic theory, with rhetoric, to logic did not readily yield to the study of poetry for itself, where the *Ars Poetica* of Horace was not concerned. In the Dantesque tradition, the *Poetics*, probably unknown to Boccaccio, is obscurely alluded to in Petrarch, and Benvenuto's commentary (c. 1376–9) on the *Divina Commedia* cites Averroes' abridgment.

A century later, Politian owns a manuscript of the *Poetics*, and shows an acquaintance (1483) with the Greek text. The number of Renaissance manuscripts yet surviving indicates that the work was accessible to his contemporaries, to whom, as to their followers in the sixteenth century, it must have seemed one that had been long neglected.

With Politian, then, begins the recorded modern study of the *Poetics* in Greek. While the Aldine Aristotle (1495–8), perhaps still reflecting the thirteenth-century preoccupation with the other works, did not include the *Poetics*, in 1498 there was printed a Latin translation by Georgio Valla, and therewith the treatise was open to the learned world. Judged by present standards, Valla's rendering was not too scholarly, nor done from the best available manuscript; but we should not estimate Renaissance scholarship by later standards which its pioneering efforts alone made possible. At length, in 1508, appeared the *editio princeps* of the Greek text, with that of the *Rhetoric*, in volume 1, as usually reckoned, of the Aldine *Rhetores Græci*. Notwithstanding the corruptions, probably due to the editor, Demetrius Ducas, the prestige of an Aldine made this the accepted text of the *Poetics* (challenged only in Morel's edition, Paris, 1555, and Tyrwhitt's, Oxford, 1794) down into the nineteenth century. The Greek treatise was first included with the complete works in 1531, in the Basel edition, supervised by Erasmus; the second Aldine edition of Aristotle, 1551–3, contained it, and likewise Silburg's edition, Frankfort, 1584–7.

Probably no Greek book save the New Testament has been so often printed as the *Poetics*. It has appeared sometimes alone, sometimes with the *Rhetoric,* sometimes with the *Ars Poetica* and Longinus *On the Sublime.* After 1508 there might be mentioned the Venetian editions of 1523, 1536, 1546, 1551; Robortelli's, 1548; Leyden, 1548; Paris, 1555 (Morel's); Florence, 1560, 1564 (Victorius'); Venice, 1572; Paris, 1630; Oxford, 1760; Göttingen, 1764 (Buhle's); Leipsic, 1786 (Reiz's); Oxford, 1794 (Tyrwhitt's). In noting these few we have not specified translations and commentaries. Pazzi's text of 1536 accompanied a revised Latin translation. Robortelli's thin folio of 1548, the first critical edition, included a Latin translation and a learned commentary. The next year came

B. Segni's Italian version, the first translation into any modern tongue; the book could now be read by those who had little or no classical learning. From this point on, to list the texts, translations, and commentaries, and discussions of passages in the work, would require an ample bibliography.

Even the Italian commentaries [11] must here be cursorily dealt with. The first to be published, Robortelli's (1548), was by a vigorous scholar, now in mid-career, who six years later brought out the *editio princeps* of Longinus *On the Sublime,* and who in the course of his life (1516–67) held professorships at Lucca, Pisa, Venice, Padua, and Bologna. But as early as 1540, Lombardi had intended to lecture on the *Poetics* before an Academy at Padua; his death prevented this. Before 1543 it was a regular academic exercise to compare a Greek tragedy and a Senecan, with the demands of the *Poetics* as a standard. Yet Maggi is said to have been the first actually to interpret the work in public, certainly before April, 1549. Its influence may be partly gathered from the file of commentators, with their dates of composition or publication: Cintio, 1543; Robortelli, 1548; Maggi and

Lombardi, 1550; Maggi (alone) 1550; Muzio, 1551; Lionardi, 1554; Capriano, 1555; Fracastoro, 1555; Caro, 1558; Bernardo Tasso, 1559; Minturno, 1559 (also 1564); Vettori (Victorius), 1560; Partenio, 1560; Scaliger, 1561; Trissino, 1563; Speroni, 1565; Piccolomini, 1575; A. Segni, 1581; Patrizzi, 1586; Denores, 1587; Rossi, 1590; Varchi, 1590; Riccoboni, 1591; Summo, 1600. Castelvetro (1570) I reserve till later. There are also unpublished commentaries among the manuscripts in the Italian libraries. One important treatise, Beni's, was published in 1613. Galluzzi's (1621) may have been read by Milton.

Had the Italian scholars no interest outside their arts of poetry and discussions of Aristotle? We must view this activity in perspective. In other fields we see a like fecundity, as witness books on courtesy, books on pastimes, editions of Greek and Latin poets—all the varied labors of the Renaissance. Nor were the arts of poetry altogether based on Aristotle. Horace was eagerly studied; while later commentators borrowed from earlier, notably from Scaliger and Castelvetro. Not all these writers would accept the alleged opinions of Aristotle in the face of 'reason.' And moral issues were potent. In addition to Horatian influences, the *Poetics* had to overcome a strong mediæval and ancient Platonic tradition in the fifteenth, and even the sixteenth century. The Platonic Socrates, objecting to epic and dramatic poetry as falsely imitative, would banish from his Utopia all literature that had no positive moral value. That poetry should please, but in any event must instruct, an Alexandrian as well as Socratic doctrine, is almost the contention of Horace.

Horace also was a conservative Roman; and the classical Renaissance is essentially Latin. It is moral, rhetorical, Ciceronian. Try as they might, the Italians could not be Greek. Dante, in spirit a Roman, takes Virgil for his guide, and the Renaissance sees in Virgil the ideal poet. So the commentators on the *Poetics,* though modern scholarship is heavily indebted to them, remained at heart Horatian. Yet thanks to the persisting mediæval subordination of poetics to logic, they rationalized poetic theory to an extent undreamed of even by Aristotle; the tendency may be seen in writers already mentioned above. The Horatian view may, however, be noted in an author preceding any of these, namely, Vida, in whose *Ars Poetica* we likewise find Quintilian's *Education of an Orator* adapted to the training of a Roman Catholic prince. Vida's poem, published in 1527, was written some years before (?1520) at Rome, in the days of Leo X. Daniello's *Poetica* (1536) contains the first modern reference to Aristotle's principle of imitation, a dozen years before Robortelli, but shows an imperfect understanding of the principle; Daniello is Horatian. The *Ars Poetica* was translated into Italian by Dolce in 1535, and into French by Pelletier in 1545.

Vida's versified treatise was the precursor of many imitations of Horace, including Boileau's *L'Art Poétique* (1674), Pope's *Essay on Criticism* (1711), and Byron's *Hints from Horace* (1811). From Daniello down, the Aristotelian and Horatian streams run side by side, sometimes distinct, but usually commingling, and frequently joined by rills from Plato and the essay of the Platonizing 'Longinus' *On the Sublime*. The mutual influence or antagonism of these traditions would require an elaborate discussion; the subject possibly is too complex to be resolved.

The effect of the *Poetics* on literature is

further complicated by the Christian tradition. In epic poems like Vida's *Christiad*, classical theories are applied to Biblical subjects, with modifications derived from Homer, Virgil, Dante, Petrarch, and others. This Continental, Christian tradition includes the various models that have been suggested for *Paradise Lost* and *Paradise Regained;* to the Continental epics one must add the Biblical plays, originating in the mediæval religious drama, but taking on a scholarly cast in Renaissance Italy, Holland, or Germany, often directly constructed upon Aristotelian principles, and fashioned after Greek or Senecan standards. Such were the *Adamus Exsul* (1600) of Grotius, the *Adamo* (1613) of Andreini, and the *Lucifer* (1654) of Vondel. The epics of Milton, and his *Samson Agonistes*, owe a general debt to the Continental movement rather than special debts to putative 'sources.'

In Italian dramatic literature Aristotle's influence is apparent a century before Andreini, and some years before Cintio noted (1543) that the comparison of the *Poetics* with Greek and Senecan tragedy was a regular university exercise. Trissino's *Sophonisba* (1515), Rucellai's *Rosmunda* (1516), and many other tragedies, were written in accordance with Aristotelian principles, as the prefaces often testify. As Italian learning spread northward, this tendency went with it; so we have prefaces and plays by Grotius and other Dutch writers, and Milton's *Of that sort of Dramatic poem which is call'd Tragedy,* prefixed to *Samson Agonistes* (1671).

The supremacy of Aristotle as a philosopher had been challenged in the Middle Ages by Duns Scotus and Abelard. In Dante's *Paradiso* the Aristotelian Aquinas is balanced by the Platonic or Neoplatonic Bonaventura. The Renaissance, assuming that Aristotle had been a 'dictator' in the Schools, denied his infallibility. But as his despotism in philosophy waned under the assaults of Bruno, Galileo, and Francis Bacon, he entered into a new dictatorship in literary criticism. In 1439 Filelfo had written: 'To defend Aristotle and the truth seems to me one and the same thing.' In 1536, however, at the University of Paris, Peter Ramus victoriously defended the thesis that 'The utterances, one and all, of Aristotle are false, and vain imaginations.' In that same year was issued Pazzi's edition of the *Poetics,* with a Latin translation; and the younger Pazzi declared that 'the precepts of poetic art are treated by Aristotle as divinely as he has treated every other branch of learning.' The date, accordingly, has been regarded as a turning-point. But the matter is not so simple. In 1555 Fracastoro likened the importance of the *Poetics* to that of Aristotle's philosophical works; and the Council of Trent, 1545–63, in sanctioning the Aristotelian philosophy, put it on a footing with Roman Catholic dogma. On the other hand, Bruno belittled the *Poetics* in 1585, and Patrizzi attacked both it and other works of Aristotle in 1586 and 1591 respectively. Patrizzi is as harsh as Ramus. The well-read Ben Jonson, writing after 1605, sounds like Bacon: 'Nothing is more ridiculous than to make an author a dictator, as the Schools have done Aristotle'; but again, now paraphrasing Heinsius, Jonson says: 'Aristotle was the first accurate critic and truest judge, nay, the greatest philosopher the world ever had.' For two centuries the authority of Aristotle and Horace reigned in literary criticism from Italy to England, thanks in part to J. C. Scaliger (1484–1558). For him, Aristotle is 'our emperor, perpetual dictator in all the arts.'

Scaliger's great work (1561), known through many editions, was an encyclopædia of poetics for France, Germany, the Netherlands, and England. In 1560 Partenio had said that all matters relating to tragedy and epic poetry had been settled by Aristotle and Horace. In 1756 Warton likened the force of the *Poetics* to that of Euclid. Lessing assailed the French for their mistakes regarding the *Poetics*, yet he, too, considered the treatise 'as infallible as the *Elements* of Euclid.'

Throughout this period, however, it was not Aristotle who was made literary dictator, but Aristotle as interpreted by Italians under the influence of Horace and of each other. Such men as A. Piccolomini, Beni, and, above all, Scaliger and Castelvetro, exercised the authority attributed to the *Poetics*.

Scaliger, the champion of Cicero in prose, and of Virgil against Homer, as a child of the Renaissance is a Roman, and not a Greek. His *Poetics*, a vast handbook, often takes issue with Aristotle, whose doctrines appear beside those of Horace. All the types of poetry and their subject-matter are described; Greek and Roman poets are compared; and the ages of Latin poetry are retailed, down to

the author's own time. With materials gar-
nered from classical and post-classical sources,
Scaliger aims at a complete encyclopædia of
his subject; Book 7 is a medley of residual
topics. The aim at sweeping inclusiveness,
the detailed comparison of Homer and Virgil,
and the award of the palm to Virgil, are
characteristic of the new learning.

The Italian study of Aristotle had very
great significance for the drama and literary
criticism of other nations. An account of the
Italian influence in France, or even upon
Corneille and Racine, would far outrun our
space. When the French dramatists went
astray, they were misled, not by Aristotle, but
by his Italian commentators, or by French
scholars who studied these. Yet the Italians,
and Scaliger not least among them, did a great
constructive work.

The most notable, however, was Lodovico
Castelvetro,[12] whose interpretation of the
Poetics had a value for Milton, and remains
illuminating not merely for historical reasons.
He was, says Rapin, 'the most subtle of all
the commentators.' Scaliger, born in 1484,
matured while Horace was ascendant. With
Castelvetro, born at Modena in 1505, and

maturing in 1536, Horace is dethroned, Plato is almost dethroned, and Aristotle becomes supreme, while Italian replaces Latin as the critic's own medium of expression. He studied at the universities of Bologna, Ferrara, Padua, and Siena. His father desiring a diplomatic career for him, the son took a degree in law; but renouncing the chance of preferment at Rome, he returned to a group of like spirits at Siena, and pursued literature in Latin, Greek, and Italian. At Modena a sharp illness, aggravated by incessant study, undermined his health, without impairing his scholarly ardor. 'He could not restrain himself from his studies,' says Muratori, 'especially that of the vulgar tongue.' He became the leader of a virtual Academy, which grew out of a kind of family life into a numerous society, enthusiastic for ancient literature, science, and diverse forms of literary criticism. Such bodies were common in Italy. At Florence a century later, Milton 'contracted an intimacy with many persons of rank and learning, and was a constant attendant at their literary parties— a practice which prevails there, and tends so much to the diffusion of knowledge and the preservation of friendship'; they still discussed

Castelvetro on the *Poetics;* the book may well
have been among those that Milton shipped
home from Venice. His unvarnished criticism
brought upon Castelvetro the enmity of a poet-
aster, Caro, a false accusation of heresy, and
threats of torture from the Inquisition. He
fled in 1560, was excommunicated, and spent
his last ten years in exile at Chiavenna, Lyons,
and Vienna. To his patron, the Emperor
Maximilian II, he dedicated in 1570 his *Poetica
d' Aristotele vulgarizzata et sposta,* contain-
ing the Greek text in short sections, with an
Italian abstract, translation, and commentary
interlarded. The Vienna edition was followed
in 1576 by that of Basel; meanwhile (1571)
Castelvetro had died.

We can but lightly touch on a few aspects of
his copious interpretation. The Italians generally misunderstood Aristotle's 'imitation,'
confusing it with the Platonic notion, or asso-
ciating it with Horace's 'Let your models be
the writers of Greece'—but substituting the
writers of Rome. Vida urges the budding
poet to copy Virgil, to pillage the ancients.
Not so Castelvetro, who understands Aristotle
almost as well as we do.

The Italians generally, lauding Virgil, upheld

the superiority of the epic poem; so Minturno, and likewise Torquato Tasso in his *Discourses* (1587); the Italian view may have decided Milton against the dramatic form for *Paradise Lost*. Castelvetro sides with Aristotle in maintaining that tragedy is the superior form, but goes beyond him by contending that poetry should give pleasure to the masses.

The Italians generally adopted the Horatian formula that the end of poetry is to profit and delight; the notion recurs in Sidney's 'delightful teaching.' As for Aristotle's catharsis of fear and pity, they thought it, not a purge, but a purification, an *expiatio* or *lustratio*, tending to ennoble the spectator. Milton, perhaps following Galluzzi, recognizes the purgative function of tragedy, but, inconsistently, aims at moral improvement as well as delight. For Castelvetro the aim of tragedy is pleasure alone; he understands by catharsis an expulsion (*scacciamento*), considers it useful and moral, not pleasure-giving, and hence, opposing Aristotle, rejects it.

Three very noticeable gifts of Castelvetro and his fellows to Renaissance criticism were the doctrines of 'decorum,' 'verisimilitude,' and the 'unities.'

[113]

The doctrine of 'decorum,' growing out of Aristotle's demand that tragic character should be 'good,' 'true to type,' 'true to life,' and 'self-consistent,' drew to itself other elements from the *Poetics:* the character should suit the action, and the parts of this should suit each other—all should be *appropriate*. Reinforced by Horatian maxims, and by the counsels of Roman rhetoric, the doctrine becomes an art of poetry in itself. Decorum, says Milton, 'is the grand masterpiece to observe.'

The doctrine of 'verisimilitude' arose from injunctions like that regarding truth to life in the delineation of character, from Aristotle's theorem that art imitates nature, and from the *'ut pictura poesis'* of Horace—or of Plutarch and Simonides. The Italians erroneously supposed that art must observe, not merely the essentials, but the details, of life, as if poetry and the stage were not subject to laws of their own in the selection and treatment of detail.

This error becomes evident in the doctrine of the three 'unities.' In respect to unity Aristotle demanded only that organic oneness which is vital to a work of art. This is the unity of action. The so-called 'unity of time' is not his, but is related to his remark that the dramatists of his generation tried 'to confine the action within the limits of one revolution of the sun.' And he says nothing that could be twisted into a 'unity of place.' The Italians may have deduced this third 'unity' from the other two, from the practice in most, but not all, of the extant Greek tragedies, and especially from the usage in Græco-Roman comedy. We are not sure how the 'unities' of time and place got a footing in criticism; but the doctrine of 'verisimilitude' made them thrive. On a stage that is true to life, it was held, the action represented should not occupy more time than such events would consume in reality; and the stage being one place, the action should occur in one place.

The unity of time first appears in Giraldi Cintio, who identifies 'one revolution of the sun' with 'a single day.' Robortelli understood the phrase to mean an artificial day of twelve hours, Segni a natural day of twenty-four. Castelvetro it was (followed by the Frenchman De la Taille in 1572) who distinctly formulated the unities. He is troubled, however, by the twelve hours. With our bodily needs and daily habits, could spectators hold out so long? In Milton's time Italian scholars still won-

[115]

dered what Aristotle meant by limiting tragedy to one day.

Such were the 'rules' that Italy gave to French criticism and the European drama; and yet not Italy alone, for Renaissance scholarship was cosmopolitan. Spanish, French, and Dutch scholars belong to the same movement. Still Italy was the cradle, and long remained the focus, of critical learning; it is fair to credit her with the spread of the Aristotelian 'rules.' Under these must be classed both the principles actually found in the *Poetics*, though sometimes imperfectly grasped, and gratuitous additions like the 'unity of place.' Aristotle argues that the hero, granted the tragic flaw, should be inwardly noble; the Renaissance infers that the hero should possess the outward trappings of nobility. Aristotle says nothing, and knows nothing, of 'five acts'; this Horatian requirement nevertheless becomes one of the 'rules,' along with the arbitrary exclusion of a fourth person in the dialogue. That 'rules' may cramp genius is evident in the struggles of Corneille and Racine with the 'unities' of place and time, and in their excuses when they disobey the 'laws.'

The French and Italian critics are often

blamed for the harm done to the drama by their Aristotelian 'rules,' and much blame has extended to Aristotle himself because of modern critics who fail to distinguish vital principles from casual observations in the *Poetics*, and because of the un-Aristotelian accretions we have noted. This hostile criticism is mostly beside the point, and neglects the positive debt of modern times to Renaissance scholarship. What the Italians did for classical authors in general, they did for Aristotle and the *Poetics*, working with industry, intelligence, and enthusiasm, and making possible the advances that have since come about in our understanding of the treatise. From our lack of perspective we are prone to exaggerate the attention given by a Scaliger or a Castelvetro to a matter like the unities of time and place. In Castelvetro the topic is but one out of a thousand, on most of which he is right; and even when wrong, he is usually suggestive. Moreover, the cramping effect of Italian criticism upon literary genius is overestimated, and its wholesome regulative influence unnoticed. Mediæval literature tends to be formless, garrulous, fragmentary. Renaissance criticism put a form upon that indigest. It taught writers the law of organic unity, the need of a beginning, middle, and end, the wisdom of dramatic economy. It is a question how much Shakespeare knew about 'the rules' till near the end of his career; but he could not have been produced without the Italian dramatists and critics, his forerunners, who studied Aristotle, and diffused the knowledge of classical drama that was in the air. Milton's epics and his tragedy both presuppose the Italian study of the *Poetics*. We may wish that the commentators had been Greek rather than Roman in their leanings, and had popularized the treatise more as a body of principles to be assimilated, and less as a set of rules to be obeyed. But instead of detracting from their immense service, or condemning them outright, one should study and respect them. The modern dramatist could still read them with profit.

Their additions to the Greek poetic theory were not all amiss. Thus Trissino, in dealing with comedy, aimed to supply what was wanting in the *Poetics*. We must allude also to Scaliger's notion, half-Christian, half-Platonic, yet tainted with Renaissance pride and self-sufficiency, that the poet is another God, and creates. Finally, to the list of effective dra-

matic characters the Italians added that of the
saint or martyr, a type not tragic in Aristotle's
sense. The death of such a person is an apparent downfall, but a real triumph, and pro-
duces in the audience a feeling of exaltation
the pagan world could never know. Aristotle
could not reckon with the situation—the nearest approach to it in Greek tragedy is offered
by the *Œdipus at Colonus*—but it may well
have the noblest dramatic effect of all.

X. THE POETICS IN SPAIN AND FRANCE

THE mediæval abridgment by Averroes was again translated in 1550 by the Spanish Jew Mantinus, but space precludes our adding much about the *Poetics* in Spain during the Renaissance. Here as elsewhere in Europe, Italian criticism was influential. Sepúlveda (after 1549) can not have preceded Robortelli in taking 'one revolution of the sun' to mean twelve hours; but Scaino, in elucidating the *Politics*, may have been the first to interpret the catharsis as a purgation rather than a purification. Of a notable triad, Pinciano, in his *Filosofía Antigua Poética* (1596), though not without some independence, is indebted to the Italians; Cascales (1617), a disciple of Castelvetro, recommends the study of other Italian critics as well; and González de Salas shows originality in his *Nueva Idea de la Tragedia Antigua* (1633). We shall hereafter refer to Vives (1492–1540), a pupil of Erasmus, active as a teacher in France, England, and the Netherlands.

In Spain, as in Italy, the Horatian cult flourished before the Aristotelian, and the notion long prevailed, too, that a play must be written in verse. Cervantes at length remarked, after Scaliger, that an epic might be written in prose as well as verse. Yet the Italians did not escape from the un-Aristotelian obsession regarding metre till the time of Beni. In France it was Molière who freed himself and the drama from the invariable constraint of metre.

The Greek text of the *Poetics* was published at Paris in 1541. We must hasten over the French commentators, without even distinguishing Aristotelian from Horatian elements in Jodelle (1552); De la Taille (1572), who died in 1608; Vauquelin de la Fresnaye (1605); Mairet (1635); La Mesnardière (1635), who betrays both Italian and Dutch influence; Chapelain (b. 1595, d. 1674), well-read in Italian criticism; D'Aubignac (1657); Pierre Corneille—for example, in his *Discours des Trois Unités* (1660); Rapin (1674); Boileau (1674).

Racine (1639–99), the outstanding 'classical' tragic poet of France and of modern times, founded his art upon the systems of D'Au-

bignac and Corneille, occasionally citing Heinsius and Aristotle himself. He follows the
'rules,' studies 'the ancients,' and observes the
principles of universal 'reason.' In forming
his plots he is eclectic; for the story of Iphigenia he consults Æschylus, Sophocles, Lu-
cretius, Horace, Euripides, Ovid, Stesichorus,
Pausanias, and Homer; he sifts his materials.
He is more creative than Corneille, perhaps
more so than any other modern writer who has
professed to cultivate classical tragedy save
Milton; his originality may be seen, for example, in his expansion of themes from the
Bible. He differs from the Attic poets, however, in elaborating the representation of love
as a dramatic motive. His Prefaces are a defence of his own method, but give no systematic
account of his theory and practice. Still they
let us see that his model is not Sophocles, the
first choice of Aristotle, but rather the roman-
tic Euripides. Thus he is typical of modern
classicism. Goethe will extol Sophocles, but
when he comes to write a classical tragedy, he
also takes Euripides as his model. Like Euripides, Racine is in substance pathetic rather
than tragic, but, as Aristotle notes of Euripides,
is tragic in his inclination toward disastrous

endings. In his Preface to *La Thébaïde* he says: 'The catastrophe of my piece is perhaps a little too bloody; in fact, scarcely an actor appears in it who does not die at the close.'

The separate effects upon Corneille and Racine of Aristotle, Horace, Italian and French and other Continental critics, translations and imitations of Seneca, and Greek tragedy, it is impossible to calculate. In Corneille the unity of place is losing its grip. He would let the scene range within the limits of a city, and wishes the dramatist had six more hours than the twenty-four that he thinks were enjoined by Aristotle. The authority of Aristotle was debated also in the quarrel between the 'ancients' and the 'moderns'—a subject too ample for our consideration. Molière, a modern, yet truly classical, finds what is good in Aristotle and Horace to be at one with his own sound sense, which he follows; he appears to have assimilated matters of value from the critics. In condemning arbitrary criticism he falls short of Saint-Evremond (1610–1703), who in later years declared: 'You are right, Gentlemen, in deriding the dreams of Aristotle and Horace, the reveries of Heinsius and Grotius, the caprices of Corneille and Ben Jonson, the fantasies of Rapin and Boileau.'

XI. THE POETICS IN THE NETHERLANDS AND GERMANY

A refugee in Holland and England, Saint-Evremond lets one see that Aristotelian criticism is cosmopolitan, and that its centre has shifted from Italy to the North. Seventeenth-century Dutch scholars [13] perhaps led in utilizing and disseminating the *Poetics*. The shift runs parallel with a better understanding of Greek literature, and with a change in the Renaissance, which has become less characteristically Latin—a process reaching to our own day. Grotius, while writing the best of Latin verse, sees the pre-eminence of Greek tragedy and of the *Poetics;* in his translation of Euripides' *Phœnissœ* he calls Aristotle *'optimus magister.'* In Italy the arguments, sometimes nearly balanced, in the main favored Virgil and epic poetry; in France the Pléiade longed for a great national epic; yet in France as well as Holland it was rather tragedy that flourished, partly under the influence of the Dutch scholar Heinsius. The Dutch, of course, read the Italian critics. The great poet Vondel (1587–1679) knew the commentaries of Robortelli, Maggi and Lombardi, and Castelvetro. But Vondel read the *Poetics* itself, at least in Latin; on the unity of action, on tragic character, on recognition and reversal, he consulted Aristotle at first hand. The vogue of Scaliger is seen when his definition of tragedy is quoted by Vondel on a par with that in the *Poetics.* Nevertheless, in Holland as elsewhere, the direct influence of Aristotle in the seventeenth century is less apparent than that of Horace: the poets aimed at a mixture of utility with delight. In the countries of the Reformation the desire for moral improvement through the drama is shown in the popularity of Biblical subjects—in Grotius' *Adamus Exsul,* for instance. Greek, Roman, and Christian themes run side by side, or intermix. In 1671 Jacob Vinck translates Euripides' *Hippolytus* into Dutch, with certain liberties which he defends by appealing to Aristotle; in 1684 Pieter Langedult gives us the play, *Christ Suffering and Glorified.* The Netherlands were touched by learning from every side, from Italy, France, Germany, and England. Rodenburg's *Eglentiers Poëtens Borst-weringh,* based upon

Sidney's *Defense of Poesy*, transmits Aristotle and Italian criticism indirectly enough. The leading student of the *Poetics* in the Netherlands, however, was Daniel Heinsius, whose work (1611) vies in eminence with that of Scaliger and Castelvetro up to the time of Dryden and Rymer; thereafter, in England, we detect the influence of Corneille and Rapin. With Heinsius should be mentioned G. J. Vossius and his treatises on poetry (1647). D'Aubignac advises the dramatist to study Aristotle, Horace, Castelvetro, Vida, Heinsius, Vossius, and Scaliger, 'of whom not a word should be lost.' But there were earlier influences in England, where the *Poetics* became known, if not through Erasmus of Rotterdam, or his pupil the Spaniard Vives, then through German rhetoricians and theorists on education like Johann Sturm.

Aside from the mediæval translation of Averroes by Hermann, the first allusion to the *Poetics* by a German writer has been found in Luther's *Address to the Christian Nobles* (1520), as the first appearance of the Greek text in a collective edition of Aristotle was at Basel in 1531. In the same year Erasmus, who supervised that edition, mentions the treatise in a letter; his writings betray no interest in the *Poetics*, but his edition had great prestige north of the Alps, and no part of it would escape notice in Germany, in the Netherlands, or in England. In 1534 Camerarius, commenting on Sophocles, models a definition of tragedy after that of the *Poetics*, yet tinged with the mediæval conception. Bucer, writing at Cambridge before 1551, mentions the Aristotelian 'reversals of fortune.' Melanchthon, like Erasmus, is concerned with rhetoric and education; for him the end of tragedy is to force rude and savage souls into moderation, to strike whole audiences with horror and move them to pity. There is a suggestion of the medical catharsis, not purification, in Hans Sachs (1560)[14]—whether a chance intuition, or gathered from an Italian treatise or the like, we can not say. Schosser's *Disputationes de Tragœdia* (1569) is based on the *Poetics*. Of the German educational leaders, Sturm (1507–89), humanist, rhetorician, student of Cicero and Horace, was also important for the study of Greek; we must return to him in connection with Ascham. Toward the end of the sixteenth century Italian criticism was well-known in Germany; in the seventeenth, the work of Heinsius and Vossius, and of the Roman Jesuit Alexander Donatus (1631), was popular. The dramatist Gryphius (1650) is exceptional for his pathological interpretation of the catharsis, possibly borrowed from Galluzzi or some other Italian. By 1700 the emotional aim of poetry was admitted, though down to Lessing, and even by him, the ethical aim is recognized. Both he and Goethe, however, realize that the end of tragedy is an emotional effect; the *prodesse* of Horace has yielded to his *delectare*—the essential position of Aristotle is now maintained.

XII. THE POETICS IN ENGLAND

AFTER Roger Bacon's reference to Hermann, in the thirteenth century, the next distinct allusion to the *Poetics* in England occurs in Bucer's *De Honestis Ludis,* a part of his *De Regno Christi,* which was presented to the youthful king Edward VI in 1551 (published at Basel in 1557). The German Reformer, then at Cambridge, recommends Biblical subjects for tragedy—divine and heroic personages, and events contrary to expectation. He quotes Aristotle's word *peripeteias* (reversals), but with him the purpose of the drama is edification. The study of the *Poetics* no doubt had already begun at Cambridge. Among his friends, Sir John Cheke, who became Regius Professor of Greek in 1540, expounded Sophocles. The influence of Vives and Sturm must also be reckoned with. The first extended treatment in English of certain ideas of Plato and Aristotle—for instance, that of 'imitation' —is found in *A Rich Storehouse or Treasurie for Nobilitye and Gentlemen* (1570), trans-

[129]

lated by 'T. B., Gent.' from Sturm's *Nobilitas Literata*. But Ascham's posthumous *Scholemaster* (1570) gives a picture of Cambridge at least twenty years before that. When he first went thither (about 1530), Ascham says, students read Aristotle's precepts without adding examples, but Redman, Cheke, Smith, Haddon, and Watson introduced a better practice: 'In tragedies . . . the Grecians Sophocles and Euripides far over match our Seneca in Latin, namely in Οἰκονομίᾳ *et Decoro*. . . . Whan M. Watson in S. John's College at Cambridge wrote his excellent tragedie of *Absalon*, M. Cheke, he, and I, for that part of trew imitation, had many pleasant talkes togither in comparing the preceptes of Aristotle, and Horace *De Arte Poetica*, with the examples of Euripides, Sophocles, and Seneca. . . . Some in England, moe in France, Germanie, and Italie also, have written tragedies in our tyme; of the which not one, I am sure, is able to abyde the trew touch of Aristotle's preceptes and Euripides' examples, save onely two that ever I saw, M. Watson's *Absalon* and Georgius Buckananus' *Jepthe*.' Sir John Redman, Sir John Cheke, Sir Thomas Smith, Walter Haddon, and Thomas Watson probably came to know the

Poetics through Bucer and Sturm, Queen Eliza-
beth through her tutor, Ascham. How soon
Italian commentaries reached England we can
not say; Erasmus' edition of Aristotle doubtless preceded them. Learning spread in various ways. Ships plying between Italy and
London carried books from the Italian presses
as ballast. Scholars like Erasmus traveled
much, and corresponded more; Ascham and
Sturm exchanged letters. The exiled Cheke
lectured for a while at Padua. Buchanan, a
Scotchman, may have first studied the *Poetics*
in France or Italy.

However the Italian theories came in, the
first direct reference to Scaliger on Aristotle
is in Sir Philip Sidney's *Defense of Poesy*,
composed between 1580 and 1583, after Sidney
had visited Padua, Paris, Vienna, and the
Netherlands. At Vienna he could hardly
escape seeing the notable work of Castelvetro.
His fascinating essay amalgamates Horace and
Aristotle with Italian Platonism and literary
criticism: 'Poesie . . . is an arte of imitation, for so Aristotle termeth it in his word
mimesis, that is to say, a representing, counter-
fetting, or figuring foorth; to speak meta-
phorically, a speaking picture; with this end,

[131]

to teach and delight.' With regret Sidney dismisses Sackville and Norton's *Gorboduc*, which might be a model for all time of Senecan tragedy, lofty, moral, delightfully instructive, were it not 'faulty both in time and place'; 'for where the stage should always represent but one place, and the uttermost time presupposed in it should be, both by Aristotle's precept and common reason, but one day, there is both many days and many places, inartificially imagined.' On the relation of poetry to history his doctrine is sound: 'Aristotle himselfe . . . plainly determineth this question, saying that poetry is . . . more philosophical and more studiously serious than history. His reason is, because poesy dealeth with . . . the universal consideration, and the history with . . . the particular.' For 'pity and fear' Sidney uses 'admiration and commiseration,' whereas Spenser (1591) writes (*Ruines of Time* 579) 'distraught twixt feare and pity'; the history of these terms from Italy down would fill a volume. Sidney's Italian parallels have never been exhaustively studied; besides Scaliger he probably read Castelvetro, and perhaps Varchi and Minturno. Tasso he may have met. According to Spingarn,[15] 'There is not an essential principle in the *Defense of Poesy* which can not be traced back to some Italian treatise on the poetic art.'

Sidney, ushering in the great age of Elizabethan poetry, must have been read by Shakespeare's friends and contemporaries, often with the Italian critics, and sometimes with the *Poetics* itself; Jonson, however, is mainly dependent upon the interpretation of Heinsius. Shakespeare did not escape the current talk about the 'unities.' There is an allusion to the unity of time, and to dramatic 'law' and 'custom,' in the Prologue to *Henry V* (1599); while Polonius (*Hamlet* 2.2) prates technically of 'scene individable, or poem unlimited,' mentions Seneca and Plautus, stock examples for the theorists, and says of the actors: 'For the law of writ and the liberty, these are the only men.' Time, the Chorus, in *The Winter's Tale* (?1610), says (Act 4): 'It is in my power to o'erthrow law.' The 'laws' of place and time in this 'poem unlimited' are manfully overthrown by an artist who regards action as the important thing. In Shakespeare's last play, however, *The Tempest* (?1611), we have 'scene individable,' and the action is comprised within three hours. 'It was,' says Dowden,[16] 'as if Shakespeare asserted his freedom to be regular or irregular as regards the classical custom of unity of time.' In truth, Shakespeare, though more Roman than Greek in his dramatic origins, is nearer than the formalists to Aristotle and the spirit of Greek tragedy. His friend Ben Jonson, translator of the *Ars Poetica* of Horace, is in tragedy far more like Seneca. Jonson hardly assimilated much from the *Poetics* before 1611. Some time thereafter he paraphrased bits of Heinsius, in his *Discoveries;* here, not in the English critics between Sidney and Jonson, the *Poetics* begins to be understood, and we wonder what Shakespeare might have learnt from it, could he have known it as he did Ovid, or Seneca and Plautus.

The first English scholar to work systematically with the *Poetics* was Theodore Goulston (1572–1632), whose Latin translation appeared in 1623. As a physician he renders *catharsis* by *'purgans,'* and then, in deference to the main tradition, adds *'expiansque.'* Milton is likely to have known the book, but seems not to have been interested in the *Poetics* until he went to Italy (1638–9). In *The Reason of Church-Government* (1641)

[134]

he thinks 'that what the greatest and choicest
wits of Athens, Rome, or modern Italy, and
those Hebrews of old, did for their country, I
in my proportion, with this over and above
of being a Christian, might do for mine.'
Proposing to himself an epic poem modeled
after Homer, Virgil, Tasso, and Job, Milton
considers 'whether the rules of Aristotle herein
are to be strictly kept, or nature to be followed,
which in them that know art and use judgment
is no transgression, but an enriching of art.'
In his tractate *Of Education* (1644) he con-
tends that, even before rhetoric one should
study poetry: 'I mean not here the prosody
of a verse, which they could not but hit upon
before among the rudiments of grammar; but
that sublime art which in Aristotle's *Poetics*,
in Horace, and the Italian commentaries of
Castelvetro, Tasso, Mazzoni, and others,
teaches what the laws of a true epic poem,
what of a dramatic, what decorum is—which
is the grand masterpiece to observe. This
would make them soon perceive what despic-
able creatures our common rhymers and play-
writers be, and show them what religious, what
glorious and magnificent, use might be made
of poetry, both in divine and human things.'

Milton was convinced that *Paradise Lost* and *Paradise Regained* subsequently benefited by his knowledge of Aristotle and the commentaries; the poet understood his own mind, and the gift of art to nature; modern critics, if they think that his learning warped his genius, are, not being poetically gifted, less likely to be right than he. Perhaps his best-sustained work is *Samson Agonistes*, a typical Renaissance tragedy in the purest English, not provincial but cosmopolitan, at once ancient, mediæval, modern, and Christian. Among his prefixed remarks, *Of that sort of Dramatic Poem which is call'd Tragedy*, are these: 'Tragedy, as it was antiently composed, hath been ever held the gravest, moralest, and most profitable of all other poems; therefore said by Aristotle to be of power by raising pity and fear, or terror, to purge the mind of those and such like passions—that is, to temper and reduce them to just measure with a kind of delight, stirred up by reading or seeing those passions well imitated. Nor is Nature wanting in her own effects to make good his assertion; for so in physic things of melancholic hue and quality are used against melancholy, sour against sour, salt to remove salt humors.

. . . Gregory Nazianzen, a Father of the Church, thought it not unbeseeming the sanctity of his person to write a tragedy, which he entitled *Christ Suffering*.[17] This is mentioned to vindicate tragedy from the small esteem, or rather infamy, which in the account of many it undergoes at this day with other common interludes; hap'ning through the poet's error of intermixing comic stuff with tragic sadness and gravity, or introducing trivial and vulgar persons. . . . In the modeling . . . of this poem, with good reason, the Antients and Italians are rather followed, as of much more authority and fame. . . . Division into act and scene referring chiefly to the stage, to which this work never was intended, is here omitted. It suffices if the whole drama be not found produc't beyond the fift act; of the style and uniformity, and that commonly called the plot, whether intricate or explicit, which is nothing indeed but such economy or disposition of the fable as may stand best with verisimilitude and decorum, they only will best judge who are not unacquainted with Æschylus, Sophocles, and Euripides, the three tragic poets unequaled yet by any, and the best rule to all who endeavor to write tragedy. The circumscription of time wherein the whole drama begins and ends is, according to antient rule and best example, within the space of twenty-four hours.' The scene is unchanged throughout. Milton fluctuates between the ideas of purification and purgation; but the last line of the drama is, 'And calm of mind, all passion spent.' He had perhaps studied both Goulston and Galluzzi, and partly anticipates the modern 'pathological' theory of the catharsis espoused by Weil and Bernays.

XIII. THE POETICS IN RECENT TIMES

AFTER Milton the data regarding the *Poetics* become too numerous, and their interrelations too complex, for any brief treatment. We can here mention but a few outstanding facts. The sound critical writings of Dryden, including *An Essay of Dramatic Poesy* (1668) which draws upon Corneille, should not go unmentioned. Nor should Thomas Rymer,[18] who follows Rapin, and who says (1674): 'The truth is, what Aristotle writes on this subject are not the dictates of his own magisterial will, or dry deductions of his metaphysics; but the poets were his masters, and what was their practice he reduced to principles.' And again: 'I have thought our poetry of the last age as rude as our architecture; one cause thereof might be that Aristotle's *Treatise of Poetry* has been so little studied by us. It was perhaps commented upon by all the great men in Italy before we well knew, on this side the Alps, that there was such a book in being.' Pope's reference to 'the mighty Stagirite,' in the *Essay on Criticism*, Warton calls 'a noble and just character of the first and best of critics.' The eighteenth century profited much from the study of Aristotle in France by Rapin (1674), the Abbé Bossu (1675), Madame Dacier (1692), and the Abbé Batteux (1771). Addison's essays (1712) on *Paradise Lost*, based upon the *Poetics*, had opened many eyes to the sureness and beauty of Milton's art. In the admirable construction of *Tom Jones*, Fielding utilizes Aristotelian principles as illustrated in Homer and applied to the novel. Of Lessing and Goethe in Germany we have spoken, but there is no space to deal even with Lessing's influence upon English critics—for example, upon Coleridge, who visited Germany in 1798–9. Long before this, in 1756, Warton had compared the *Poetics* to Euclid. Gray read the treatise without enthusiasm, but the poet-laureate Pye translated it (1788). An annotated translation by Twining appeared in 1789. In 1794 came the valuable edition by the mediæval and classical scholar Tyrwhitt. Dr. Johnson knew the worth of the *Poetics* when he printed Dryden's spirited marginalia on Rymer, obtained by Johnson from Garrick. Burke [19] said: 'Aristotle has spoken so much and so solidly upon the force of imitation, in his *Poetics*, that it makes any further discourse upon this subject the less necessary.'

Of the modern scholars who have helped to give us an authentic text, and an exact understanding, of the treatise, we can hardly note even the more significant. The fringes of their labor reach back to the eighteenth century, and into most of the countries of Europe. The *Poetics* has been translated into Danish, Polish, and Hungarian, and repeatedly into other languages. Notable efforts have come from England, beginning with Twining and Tyrwhitt, and coming down to Butcher, Margoliouth, and, above all, Bywater. The French, with Thurot, Nisard, Fouillée, Noël, Saint-Hilaire, Hatzfeld, and Dufour, have not been idle. Through Henri Weil we pass to Bernays and Germany, where a host of scholars, great and small, have busied themselves with the *Poetics*. In 1753 we have the German translation by M. C. Curtius, a contemporary of Lessing. Goethe brings us into the nineteenth century. Here, among the earlier names, we find Valett, E. Müller,

Gräfenhan, and Stahr. Others, as we come down, are Ritter, J. T. Mommsen, Bekker, Spengel, Forchhammer, Baumgart, Moritz Schmidt, Döring, W. Christ, Bullinger, Susemihl, and Ueberweg, whose activities overlap with those of Haidenhain, Gomperz, Feller, Diels, and a crowd of lesser men; there was a consuming interest in textual criticism, but an interest in larger questions, too. About the middle of the century, and later, there was an Egyptian plague of doctoral dissertations on the interpretation of the catharsis-clause and similar topics in the *Poetics*, while university professors scrutinized every word and phrase in the Greek text, and battled in the classical journals over meanings and emendations. Or again, a student, by way of a doctoral thesis, would test Schiller's *Braut von Messina* by Aristotelian principles, a kind of practice as old as the Italian Renaissance. Flighty guesswork was displayed, as well as critical acumen; yet the severe standards of a scholarship both minute and broad prevailed, and at length appeared the best German edition of the *Poetics*, by Johannes Vahlen (1885). The best edition thus far, however, is a product of English learning, Ingram Bywater's *Aris-*

totle On the Art of Poetry, a Revised Text, with Critical Introduction, Translation, and Commentary, Oxford, 1909. Bywater, owing much to the Germans, and to Vahlen in particular, brought to his task a knowledge of virtually all the work that had been done for the treatise from his own age and that of Tyrwhitt back to the Italians Victorius and Robortelli. Nevertheless his text, separately published in 1911, failed to profit adequately from the researches of Margoliouth into the Arabic version, which has since (1920) been restudied with great ingenuity and surprising results by Gudeman.

Of recent English poets, Wordsworth [20] at first merely heard of the treatise, probably from Coleridge: 'Aristotle, I have been told, hath said that poetry is the most philosophic of all writing. It is so: its object is truth, not individual and local, but general, and operative.' Eventually he read of 'the tragic scene' and 'pity or fear,' and agreed with Aristotle on the tragic quality of Euripides. Coleridge [21] says: 'I adopt with full faith the principle of Aristotle that poetry as poetry is essentially ideal, that it avoids and excludes all accident. . . . To this accidentality I ob-

[143]

ject, as contravening the essence of poetry, which Aristotle pronounces to be . . . the most intense, weighty, and philosophical product of human art; adding, as the reason, that it is the most catholic and abstract.' Byron, a disciple of Horace, knows the 'unities,' sometimes observes and sometimes disregards them, and draws merriment from 'Longinus o'er a bottle, or every man his own Aristotle.' Shelley's *Defence of Poetry*, written on Italian soil, is Platonic, hardly Aristotelian. Scott apologizes for his neglect of structural unity; on occasion he rebels against 'the rules.' While Ruskin shows no special acquaintance with the *Poetics*, Newman takes issue with it in a mistaken but suggestive essay. Arnold [22] in his note-books made extracts from a German commentary on what he elsewhere calls (1853) 'the admirable treatise of Aristotle'; that he had reflected on its principles is disclosed in *Merope;* but he underestimates Addison on *Paradise Lost.*

In Italy there has of late been a revival of scholarly interest in the *Poetics*. In America the text has never been edited, nor have many dissertations been written on it by students of Greek; it has been once translated,

by a teacher of English.[23]   In fact, any practical interest has been mainly evinced by students with a bias toward modern letters.   In
recent years there has been a tendency to use
it not merely as a curious historical document,
but as an instrument for the study of the ancient classical, and even of the modern, drama.
A sensible writer in the *Saturday Evening Post*
has maintained that the art of short stories is
best learned from Aristotle.

The growing attention to the *Poetics* is a
hopeful sign in an age of excessive individual-
ism; the treatise will always serve as an anti-
dote to anarchy in criticism.   Classical scholars
have perhaps tended of late to undervalue it;
in past times we have seen its doctrines, first
misinterpreted, and then mistakenly and slav-
ishly obeyed.   It has not been underrated,
however, by the best poets, or by the best
scholars such as Alfred Croiset or Bywater.
The latter says of the work and its author:
'The book, taken as it is, with perhaps an
occasional side-light from some of his other
works, is intelligible enough; after a brief
introduction, he gives in outline all that he
has to say on the subject before him, the
technique of the drama and the epic.   He tells

[145]

one, in fact, how to construct a good play and a good epic, just as in the *Rhetoric* he tells one how to make a good speech. And in doing this, he has succeeded in formulating once for all the great first principles of dramatic art, the canons of dramatic logic which even the most adventurous of modern dramatists can only at his peril forget or set at naught.'

Can the *Poetics* really be helpful to a poet? Must he not use artistic principles by instinct? We have seen Milton's answer to the question: Let the poet read Aristotle and the commentaries. Shakespeare [24] in effect answers it thus: 'Over that art which you say adds to nature is an art that nature makes.' And Ben Jonson [25] thus: 'Without art, nature can ne'er be perfect; and without nature, art can claim no being. But our poet must beware that his study be not only to learn of himself; for he that shall affect to do that confesseth his ever having a fool to his master. He must read many, but ever the best and choicest. Those that can teach him anything he must ever account his masters and reverence; among whom Horace and (he that taught him) Aristotle deserved to be the first in estimation. Aristotle was the first accurate critic and truest judge—nay, the greatest philosopher the world ever had; for he noted the vices of all knowledges, in all creatures, and out of many men's perfections in a science he formed still one art. So he taught us two offices together: how we ought to judge rightly of others, and what we ought to imitate specially in ourselves. But all this in vain without a natural wit, and a poetical nature in chief; for no man so soon as he knows this [the *Poetics*], or reads it, shall be able to write the better; but as he is adapted to it by nature he shall grow the perfecter writer.'

Wordsworth [26] speaks in the *Prelude* of 'the great Nature that exists in works of mighty poets.' It is the same power that shows itself in the work of a mighty critic like Aristotle. His treatise is one of the great constructive efforts of a scientific imagination that is own sister to the poetic genius. Says Sir Frederick Pollock:[27] 'In those branches of scientific inquiry which are most abstract, most formal, and most remote from the grasp of the ordinary sensible imagination, a higher power of imagination, akin to the creative insight of the poet, is most needed, and most fruitful of lasting work.' Some share of imagination, at

[147]

once scientific and artistic, is necessary in the man who would profit by Aristotle's treatise. But the gifted person who, through long, severe, and loving study, in time adapts his mind to the *Poetics,* until its thought becomes second nature to him—a vital principle, not an arbitrary rule—will surely be a sounder judge of poetry. If to begin with he has in sufficient measure the impulse to 'imitate,' if he has an inborn sense of harmony and rhythm, and if he has that eye for resemblances which is the source of figurative diction and the mark of genius, he likewise 'shall grow the perfecter writer.'

NOTES AND BIBLIOGRAPHY

NOTES

The plan of the series forbids an inclusion of systematic references in support of many statements in this volume. The works cited in the following Notes, or listed in the Bibliography, do not exhaust the account of the sources to which I am indebted for facts or opinions. Only a few salient references can be given.

1. 'Investigators': see Hermann Usener, *Vorträge und Aufsätze* (Leipsic, 1907), p. 83.

2. '*Tractatus Coislinianus* . . . 1839': see J. A. Cramer, *Anecdota Græca* (Oxford, 1839–41) 1.403–6.

3. 'More detail': for general readers the *Poetics* needs to be expanded, especially as regards the illustrations from the Greek poets. See my *Amplified Version* (Boston, 1913, now published by Harcourt, Brace and Company, New York).

4. '*Tractatus Coislinianus*': for details regarding this see *An Aristotelian Theory of Comedy* (New York, 1922), my companion-volume to the *Amplified Version* of the *Poetics* mentioned in Note 3.

5. 'The phrase': see *Merry Wives of Windsor* 1.3.30.

6. '*Babylonians*': see Aristotle's *Rhetoric* 3.2.15.

7. 'Wordsworth': see his Preface to *Lyrical Ballads,* 1800.

8. 'Saintsbury': see his *History of Criticism* (Edinburgh, 1900–04) 1.39, 56.

9. 'Manuscripts do': see Alfred Gudeman, 'Die Syrisch-Arabische Uebersetzung der Aristotelischen Poetik,' in *Philologus* 76 (1920). 239–65.

10. 'Tzetzes . . . on tragic poetry': see *Comicorum Græcorum Fragmenta,* ed. by Georg Kaibel (Berlin, 1899), 1.43–9.

11. 'Italian commentaries': for matters connected with the *Poetics* in Italy, and throughout the Renaissance in general, I am necessarily indebted to J. E. Spingarn's *Literary Criticism in the Renaissance* (New York, 1908), a work which has done more than any other to open up the subject.

12. 'Castelvetro': see H. B. Charlton, *Castelvetro's Theory of Poetry* (Manchester, 1913).

13. 'Dutch scholars': see A. G. van Hamel, *Zeventiende-Eeuwsche Opvattingen en Theorieën over Litteratuur in Nederland* (The Hague, 1918).

14. 'Hans Sachs (1560)': see J. E. Gillet, 'The Catharsis-Clause in German Criticism before Lessing,' in *The Journal of Philology* 35 (1920). 95–112.

15. 'Spingarn': see his *Literary Criticism in the Renaissance*, pp. 257–8.

16. 'Dowden': see his Introduction to *The Tempest*, in the three-volume edition of Shakespeare published by the Oxford University Press.

17. *'Christ Suffering':* the tragedy no longer is attributed to Gregory Nazianzen.

18. 'Rymer': see his *Tragedies of the Last Age,* in *Critical Essays of the Seventeenth Century,* ed. by J. E. Spingarn (Oxford, 1908), 2.207.

19. 'Burke': see his *Philosophical Inquiry into the Origin of our Ideas of the Sublime and Beautiful* 1.16.

20. 'Wordsworth': see his Preface to *Lyrical Ballads,* 1800; *Ecclesiastical Sonnets* 2.26; *Memoirs of William Wordsworth,* by Christopher Wordsworth (London, 1851), 2.468.

21. 'Coleridge': see his *Biographia Literaria,* ed. by J. Shawcross (Oxford, 1907), 2.33,101.

22. 'Arnold': for this and several other references I am indebted to a typewritten essay in the Cornell University Library, *The Utterances of Some English Poets on the Poetics of Aristotle* (1919), by my former pupil, Alice W. Mulhern (Mrs. Frederic H. Robinson).

23. 'Teacher of English': see Note 3.

24. 'Shakespeare': see *Winter's Tale* 4.4.90.

25. 'Ben Jonson': see his *Discoveries,* ed. by Maurice Castelain (Paris, n.d.), p. 127.

26. 'Wordsworth': see *Prelude* 5.594-5.

27. 'Pollock': see my *Methods and Aims in the Study of Literature* (Boston, 1915), p. 26.

BIBLIOGRAPHY

Strangely enough, no adequate bibliography of the *Poetics* has ever been published; the nearest approach to one is contained in M. Schwab's anastatic reproduction of his manuscript *Bibliographie d'Aristote,* Paris (Welter), 1896. Bibliographical data for the influence of the *Poetics* are found in several works cited in the preceding Notes (as Spingarn's and Saintsbury's), in Bywater's edition, and in a number of other works cited below. In my collections for the present volume I made a tentative bibliography of the *Poetics* that would fill another volume of equal or greater size; this I hope some time to improve and publish. The following list contains only a few of the more important, characteristic, or recent titles.

ADDISON, J., *Criticisms on Paradise Lost* (ed. by A. S. Cook). Boston, 1892.

BATTEUX, C., *Les Quatre Poétiques d'Aristote, d'Horace, de Vida, de Despréaux.* Paris, 1771.

BAUMGART, H., *Aristoteles, Lessing, und Goethe.* Leipsic, 1877.

BERNAYS, J., *Zwei Abhandlungen über die Aristotelische Theorie des Drama.* Berlin, 1880.

BOUCHIER, E. S., *Aristotle's Poetics.* Oxford, 1908.

BRADLEY, A. C., *Shakespearean Tragedy.* London, 1911.

BREITINGER, H., *Les Unités d'Aristote avant le Cid de Corneille.* Geneva, 1879.

BRETT, G. S., 'Some Reflections on Aristotle's Theory

of Tragedy,' in *Philosophical Essays Presented to John Watson* (Kingston, Canada, 1923), pp. 158–78.

BUTCHER, S. H., *Aristotle's Theory of Poetry and Fine Art*. London, 1920.

BYWATER, I., *Aristotle On the Art of Poetry*. Oxford, 1909.

————, 'Milton and the Aristotelian Definition of Tragedy,' in *The Journal of Philology* 27 (1901). 267–75.

COOK, A. S., *The Art of Poetry: the Poetical Treatises of Horace, Vida, and Boileau, with the Translations by Howes, Pitt, and Soame*. Boston, 1892.

DRAPER, J. W., 'Aristotelian "Mimesis" in Eighteenth-Century England,' in *Publications of the Modern Language Association of America* 36 (1921). 372–400.

DURHAM, W. H., *Critical Essays of the Eighteenth Century*. New Haven, 1905.

EGGER, A. E., *Essai sur l'Histoire de la Critique chez les Grecs*. Paris, 1887.

FRIEDLAND, L. S., 'The Dramatic Unities in England,' in *The Journal of English and Germanic Philology* 10 (1911). 56–89, 280–99, 453–67.

GAYLEY, C. M., and F. N. SCOTT, *Methods and Materials of Literary Criticism*. Boston, 1899.

————, and B. P. KURTZ, *Methods and Materials of Literary Criticism*. Boston, 1920.

GILLET, J. E., 'A Note on the Tragic "Admiratio,"' in *The Modern Language Review* 13 (1918). 233–8.

GOMPERZ, T., *Zu Aristoteles' Poetik*. Vienna, 1888.

GUDEMAN, A., *Aristoteles über die Dichtkunst*. Leipsic, 1921. (German translation of the *Poetics*.)

HAMELIUS, P., *Was Dachte Shakespeare über Poesie?* Brussels, 1898.

HOWARD, W. G., 'Ut Pictura Poesis,' in *Publications of the Modern Language Association of America* 24 1909). 40–123.

KNOKE, F., *Begriff der Tragödie nach Aristoteles*. Berlin, 1906.

LA HARPE, J. F., 'Analyse de la *Poétique* d'Aristote,' in *Cours de Littérature, Anciens* (Paris, 1800), vol. I, *Poésie,* chapter I.

LANSON, G., *Esquisse d'une Histoire de la Tragédie Française.* New York, 1920.

LEMAÎTRE, J., *Corneille et la Poétique d'Aristote.* Paris, 1888.

LESSING, G. E., *Hamburgische Dramaturgie.* Hamburg [=Bremen], 1767-9.

LUZÁN, I., *Poética.* Saragossa, 1737.

MARGOLIOUTH, D. S., *The Poetics of Aristotle, Translated from Greek into English and from Arabic into Latin, with a Revised Text.* London, 1911.

MENÉNDEZ Y PELAYO, M., *Historia de las Ideas Estéticas en España,* in his *Obras Completas.* Madrid, 1890.

MURRAY, G., 'An Essay in the Theory of Poetry,' in *The Yale Review* 10 (1921). 482-499.

NEWMAN, J. H., *Poetry, with Reference to Aristotle's Poetics* (ed. by A. S. Cook). Boston, 1891.

PRICKARD, A. O., *Aristotle On the Art of Poetry, a Lecture.* London, 1891.

ROBERTSON, J. G., 'Lessing's Interpretation of Aristotle,' in *The Modern Language Review* 12 (1917). 157-68, 319-39.

ROSTAGNI, A., 'Aristotele e Aristotelismo nella Storia dell' Estetica Antica,' in *Studi Italiani di Filologia Classica,* Nuova Serie 4 (1922). 1-147.

SAINTSBURY, G., *A History of Criticism and Literary Taste in Europe.* Edinburgh, 1900-04.

———, *Loci Critici.* Boston, 1903.

SMITH, G. G., *Elizabethan Critical Essays.* Oxford, 1904.

SPINGARN, J. E., *A History of Literary Criticism in the Renaissance.* New York, 1908.

STARKIE, W. J. M., 'An Aristotelian Analysis of "the Comic," illustrated from Aristophanes, Rabelais, Shakespeare, and Molière,' in *Hermathena,* No. 42 (1920). 26-51.

BIBLIOGRAPHY

SYMMES, H. S., *Les Débuts de la Critique Dramatique en Angleterre.* Paris, 1903.

TOFFANIN, G., *La Fine dell' Umanesimo.* Turin, 1920.

VAHLEN, I., *Beiträge zu Aristoteles' Poetik.* Leipsic, 1885.

————, *Beiträge zu Aristoteles' Poetik.* Leipsic, 1914.

VALGIMIGLI, M., *Aristotele. Poetica. Traduzione, Note, e Introduzione.* Bari, 1916.

WILLIAMS, R. C., 'The Purpose of Poetry, and particularly the Epic, as Discussed by Critical Writers of the Sixteenth Century in Italy,' in *The Romanic Review* 12 (1921). 1–20.

[157]

Our Debt to Greece and Rome

AUTHORS AND TITLES

AUTHORS AND TITLES

AUTHORS AND TITLES